TAIPEI TRAVEL

GUIDE

Exploring Taipei Rich History And Top Attractions For First Time Travelers

Sarah Wiseman

TABLE OF CONTENT

INTRODUCTION 6

    Overview of Taipei 9

    History and Culture 12

    Weather and Best Time to Visit 15

    Transportation in Taipei 18

CHAPTER 1 22

    Planning Your Trip to Taipei 22

    Visa and Entry Requirements 22

    Travel Budget and Currency 25

    Accommodation Options 28

    Packing Tips and Essential Items 32

CHAPTER 2 36

    Top Tourist Attractions 36

    Taipei 101 36

    National Palace Museum 38

    Chiang Kai-shek Memorial Hall 40

    Longshan Temple 43

Ximending 45

Elephant Mountain 48

Beitou Hot Springs 50

Maokong Gondola 52

Shilin Night Market 54

Yangmingshan National Park 57

CHAPTER 3 60

Exploring Taipei's Neighborhoods 60

Zhongzheng District 60

Wanhua District 62

Datong District 65

Xinyi District 67

Da'an District 69

Beitou District 71

Songshan District 73

CHAPTER 4 76

Cultural and Historical Sites 76

Taiwanese Temples and Religious Sites 76

Historical Landmarks and Museums 80

Traditional Taiwanese Arts and Crafts 83

Preservation and Promotion of Taiwanese Arts and Crafts .. 85

CHAPTER 5... 86

    Outdoor Activities in Taipei...................................... 86

        Hiking and Nature Trails..................................... 86

        Cycling and Biking Routes 89

        River Cruises and Boat Tours............................... 91

        Picnic Spots and Parks 93

CHAPTER 6... 98

    Culinary Delights in Taipei...................................... 98

        Iconic Taiwanese Dishes..................................... 98

        Must-Try Street Food.. 101

        Night Markets and Food Stalls 104

        Themed Restaurants and Cafes 107

CHAPTER 7.. 112

    Shopping in Taipei.. 112

        Popular Shopping Districts................................. 112

        Traditional Markets and Bazaars 115

        Trendy Boutiques and Designer Stores.............. 118

        Souvenirs and Local Crafts 121

CHAPTER 8.. 126

Nightlife and Entertainment 126

Bars and Pubs 126

Nightclubs and Dancing Venues 129

Live Music and Concerts 132

Theater and Performances 135

CHAPTER 9... 140

Practical Information and Safety Tips 140

Emergency Numbers and Healthcare................. 140

Language and Communication........................... 142

Cultural Etiquette and Customs.......................... 143

CONCLUSION 147

INTRODUCTION

Three years ago, I embarked on a life-changing trip to Taipei, Taiwan, and little did I know that it would become one of the most wonderful and unforgettable experiences of my life. From the moment I set foot in this vibrant city, I was mesmerized by its blend of modernity and traditional charm.

As I wandered through the bustling streets of Taipei, I was immediately captivated by the friendly smiles and warm greetings from the locals. Their genuine hospitality made me feel welcome and at ease, like I was part of their community. It was this warmth and openness that allowed me to immerse myself fully in the local culture and customs.

During my time in Taipei, I explored the iconic landmarks that define this unique city. Taipei 101, with its towering presence and stunning views, left me in awe of the city's impressive skyline. The National Palace Museum showcased the richness of Taiwan's history and cultural heritage, leaving me with a profound appreciation for its art and artifacts.

One of the highlights of my trip was discovering the hidden gems of Taipei's neighborhoods. Ximending's trendy streets offered a vibrant atmosphere with its street art, boutiques, and lively entertainment. The serenity of Beitou District and its soothing hot springs provided the perfect escape from the city's hustle and bustle. And the quaint alleys of Da'an District allowed me to savor the local delicacies and engage in delightful conversations with fellow travelers.

As I delved into the traditional Taiwanese arts and crafts, I found myself enchanted by the intricate details and dedication put into each piece. From witnessing the art of calligraphy to experiencing the vibrant energy of Taiwanese puppetry, I felt a profound connection to the culture that has been passed down through generations.

Taipei's natural beauty also took my breath away. I hiked up Elephant Mountain to witness a breathtaking sunset over the city, and I reveled in the tranquility of Yangmingshan National Park's lush landscapes. The Maokong Gondola ride offered a bird's-eye view of Taipei's verdant mountains, making it a serene escape from the urban buzz.

Throughout my journey, I indulged in the tantalizing Taiwanese cuisine, from iconic dishes to mouthwatering street food. The vibrant flavors of beef noodle soup, stinky tofu, and bubble tea left my taste buds dancing with delight. And the bustling night markets, such as Shilin Night Market, tempted me with a feast of delicious treats and unique souvenirs.

My time in Taipei sparked a deep passion for travel and a desire to share this extraordinary city with others. Upon returning home, I felt inspired to write a comprehensive Taipei Travel Guide to showcase the beauty and allure of this captivating destination. I wanted others to experience the warmth of its people, the richness of its culture, and the wonders that await in every corner of Taipei.

Now, as I write this story, I can't help but smile at the cherished memories that Taipei has gifted me. It wasn't just a trip; it was a transformative journey that left an indelible mark on my heart. Taipei has a way of captivating every traveler who steps foot on its soil, leaving them with a longing to return and an endless fascination for all that it offers.

If you're seeking a destination that will ignite your senses, awaken your spirit, and leave you with an experience of a lifetime, look no further than Taipei. This enchanting city will welcome you with open arms, embrace you in its rich tapestry of culture, and leave you with memories that will last a lifetime. So, don't wait any longer—come, immerse yourself in the beauty of Taipei, and let this city weave its magic around you. Your own Taipei adventure awaits!

Overview of Taipei

The energetic capital of Taiwan, Taipei, is a cutting-edge metropolis where innovation and tradition coexist together. Situated in the northern part of the island, Taipei serves as the political, economic, and cultural hub of Taiwan. With its rich history, bustling markets, stunning skyscrapers, and delectable cuisine, Taipei offers an unforgettable experience for travelers of all kinds.

The city is nestled between lush mountains, including the iconic Elephant Mountain, and the picturesque Tamsui River. Taipei boasts a unique mix of traditional Taiwanese architecture, ancient temples, and contemporary landmarks like Taipei 101, once the tallest building in the world.

1. Geography and Demographics

Taipei covers an area of approximately 271 square kilometers (104.5 square miles) and is divided into twelve administrative districts. As of the latest data, the city's population hovers around 2.7 million people, making it one of the most densely populated cities globally. The official language is Mandarin Chinese, but English is widely spoken, especially in tourist areas.

2. Economy and Industry

Taipei plays a pivotal role in Taiwan's thriving economy. It is a major financial center, housing the headquarters of numerous multinational companies. The city's industries range from technology and manufacturing to tourism and creative arts. Renowned Taiwanese companies such as ASUS, Acer, and HTC have their roots in Taipei.

3. Cultural Melting Pot

Taipei's cultural identity is a melting pot of influences from various origins. The rich indigenous heritage of Taiwan is preserved through museums and festivals that showcase traditional customs and rituals. Additionally, Taipei embraces Chinese, Japanese, and Western influences, owing to its complex historical background.

4. Urban Attractions

Travelers can delve into the city's captivating history and culture by visiting iconic landmarks like the National Palace Museum, which houses one of the most extensive collections of Chinese art in the world. Taipei 101, with its modern architecture and observatory, offers breathtaking panoramic views of the city. Chiang Kai-shek Memorial Hall, dedicated to Taiwan's former leader, is another must-visit landmark.

5. Night Markets and Culinary Delights

Taipei's night markets are a feast for the senses, offering a plethora of street food and local delicacies. Shilin Night Market, Raohe Street Night Market, and Ningxia Night Market are among the most famous. From the world-famous bubble tea to stinky tofu and xiaolongbao, Taipei's culinary offerings are diverse and irresistible.

6. Modern Art and Creativity

The city's creative spirit can be witnessed in its numerous art galleries, studios, and creative hubs. The Huashan 1914 Creative Park is a prime example, housed in a repurposed industrial space that now hosts exhibitions, design markets, and live performances. The Red House Theater, a historic landmark, is a hub for LGBTQ+ events, exhibitions, and shops.

7. Festivals and Events

Taipei celebrates various festivals throughout the year, each offering a unique cultural experience. The annual Lantern Festival, Dragon Boat Festival, and Moon Festival are celebrated with great enthusiasm, while international events like the Taipei Film Festival and Taipei Arts Festival draw visitors from all over the world.

8. Connectivity

Taipei is well-connected domestically and internationally. The Taoyuan International Airport serves as the primary gateway to the city, welcoming flights from major cities across the globe. Within the city, an extensive public transportation network, including the MRT (Mass Rapid Transit) system, buses, and taxis, ensures convenient and efficient travel.

9. Safety and Hospitality

Taipei is considered one of the safest cities in the world, with low crime rates and a welcoming atmosphere. The local people, known for their friendliness and hospitality, are eager to help travelers navigate the city and explore its treasures.

History and Culture

Taipei's history spans several centuries, shaped by a diverse array of influences and events. Understanding the city's historical context is crucial to appreciating its culture, architecture, and traditions.

1. Prehistoric Roots

The area that is now Taipei was once inhabited by the Ketagalan indigenous people, who lived in harmony with the surrounding nature. Remnants of their culture and artifacts can be found in museums and cultural centers.

2. Qing Dynasty Rule

During the Qing Dynasty, Taiwan was ceded to China and became a province. In the mid-18th century, Han Chinese settlers began arriving, establishing villages and communities that eventually grew into modern-day Taipei.

3. Japanese Occupation

Taiwan was given to Japan in 1895 as compensation for the First Sino-Japanese War. The Japanese influence left a lasting mark on Taipei's architecture and infrastructure. Many historic buildings and temples were reconstructed during this period.

4. Post-World War II and Republic of China

After World War II, Taiwan was handed back to China under the Republic of China (ROC) government. The ROC government fled to Taiwan in 1949 after the Chinese Civil War, with Taipei becoming the capital of the ROC.

5. Economic Boom and Democracy

In the latter half of the 20th century, Taiwan experienced rapid economic growth, becoming one of the "Four Asian Tigers." This economic boom transformed Taipei into a modern city with towering skyscrapers and advanced infrastructure. Alongside this growth, Taiwan transitioned to a thriving democracy, fostering freedom of expression and cultural preservation.

6. Religious and Cultural Heritage

Taiwanese culture is deeply rooted in its religious beliefs, combining Taoism, Buddhism, and Confucianism. Taipei is home to numerous temples and religious sites, such as the Longshan Temple, a 300-year-old place of worship that exemplifies the fusion of Chinese and Taiwanese culture.

7. Traditional Arts and Crafts

Artisans in Taipei continue to preserve and pass on traditional crafts like calligraphy, pottery, and paper cutting. Visiting workshops and art centers provides insight into these ancient skills.

8. Language and Cuisine

Taiwanese Mandarin is the official language, but Taiwanese Hokkien (Min Nan) is widely spoken. The vibrant culinary scene showcases diverse regional dishes, with Taiwanese snacks, street food, and night market delicacies offering a delicious culinary journey.

9. Festivals and Celebrations

Taiwanese festivals are joyous occasions, with celebrations like Chinese New Year, the Dragon Boat Festival, and the Mid-Autumn Festival being widely observed. The annual Taipei

Lantern Festival is a spectacular event that illuminates the city with colorful lantern displays.

10. Contemporary Culture

Taipei's contemporary culture is evident in its flourishing art scene, music festivals, street art, and creative spaces. The city's vibrant youth culture contributes to its dynamic and ever-evolving atmosphere.

Weather and Best Time to Visit

Understanding the climate and the best time to visit Taipei is essential for planning a comfortable and enjoyable trip. Taipei experiences a subtropical climate with distinct seasons throughout the year.

1. Seasons in Taipei

Spring (March to May): Spring is a delightful time to visit Taipei as the weather is mild and pleasant, with temperatures ranging from 15°C to 25°C (59°F to 77°F). The city is adorned with cherry blossoms, making it a picturesque sight.

Summer (June to August): Summer in Taipei can be hot and humid, with temperatures reaching 30°C to 35°C (86°F to 95°F). Occasional rainfall and typhoons are common during this season.

Autumn (September to November): Autumn is another excellent time to visit Taipei. The weather is mild, and the average temperature ranges from 20°C to 25°C (68°F to 77°F). The city's parks and natural landscapes showcase vibrant autumn colors.

Winter (December to February): Winter in Taipei is relatively mild, with temperatures ranging from 10°C to 20°C (50°F to 68°F). It rarely snows in the city, but the surrounding mountains may experience snowfall.

2. Best Time to Visit

The best time to visit Taipei largely depends on individual preferences and tolerance to weather conditions.

Spring and Autumn: These transitional seasons are generally considered the best time to visit Taipei. The weather is comfortable, and outdoor activities are enjoyable. The cherry blossoms in spring and the autumn foliage add charm to the city.

Festivals and Events: Taipei hosts several festivals and events throughout the year. If you wish to experience the grandeur of Chinese New Year, visit during late January or early February. For the exuberance of the Dragon Boat Festival, plan your trip around June. The Taipei Lantern Festival, usually held in February or March, is another major event to consider.

Low Tourist Season: If you prefer fewer crowds and lower accommodation prices, consider visiting Taipei during the winter months. While it might be cooler, you can still explore indoor attractions and enjoy the city's culinary offerings.

3. Packing Tips

Spring and Autumn: Bring light and breathable clothing with a light jacket or cardigan for cooler evenings.For touring the city, you must have good walking shoes.

Summer: Pack lightweight and loose-fitting clothing, along with sunscreen, sunglasses, and a hat to protect against the strong sun. An umbrella or raincoat can come in handy during sudden rain showers.

Winter: Layer your clothing to stay warm, and pack a medium-weight jacket. It's a good idea to have an umbrella or raincoat for occasional drizzles.

4. Tips for Coping with Weather

Stay Hydrated: Taipei's summer heat and humidity can be draining. Keep a reusable water bottle with you and sip often to remain hydrated.

Sun Protection: Apply sunscreen before heading out, wear a hat and sunglasses, and seek shade during the hottest hours of the day.

Rainy Days: Keep an umbrella or a lightweight raincoat in your bag during the wetter months to be prepared for sudden rain showers.

5. Weather and Activities

The weather can influence your activities in Taipei. During hot summer days, indoor attractions like museums and shopping malls can provide respite from the heat. In autumn, exploring parks and hiking trails becomes especially enjoyable due to the pleasant weather and stunning foliage.

Transportation in Taipei

Navigating Taipei is remarkably convenient, thanks to its well-developed and efficient transportation system. Whether you prefer public transit or private options, Taipei provides an array of choices for getting around the city and beyond.

1. Mass Rapid Transit (MRT)

The MRT is Taipei's most popular mode of transportation, known for its cleanliness, reliability, and extensive network. The system covers major areas of the city, making it easy to access tourist attractions, shopping districts, and residential neighborhoods. MRT stations are equipped with clear signage in English and Mandarin, easing navigation for international visitors.

2. Buses

Taipei's bus system complements the MRT, serving routes that may not be covered by the subway. Buses provide convenient access to various destinations, including scenic spots and suburbs. The EasyCard, a contactless payment card, can be used for both MRT and bus rides, streamlining the payment process.

3. Taiwan High-Speed Rail (THSR)

The THSR connects Taipei to other major cities in Taiwan, including Taoyuan, Taichung, Tainan, and Kaohsiung. This high-speed rail system offers a fast and efficient way to travel long distances, reducing travel times significantly.

4. Taiwan Railway Administration (TRA)

The TRA operates conventional train services, linking Taipei to various towns and cities across Taiwan. It is a great option for those looking to explore the island beyond the metropolitan area.

5. Taipei YouBike

For a more eco-friendly and active mode of transportation, Taipei's YouBike rental system is ideal. With designated bike lanes and stations throughout the city, YouBike offers an enjoyable way to explore Taipei's streets and riverside paths.

6. Taxis and Ride-Sharing

Taxis are readily available in Taipei and offer a comfortable and convenient way to travel, especially during late hours when public transit options are limited. Ride-sharing services like Uber and others also operate in the city.

7. Walking and Cycling

Taipei is a pedestrian-friendly city, and walking is an excellent way to explore its neighborhoods and alleys. With many sidewalks and pedestrian crossings, pedestrians can navigate safely through the city. Additionally, biking enthusiasts will appreciate the dedicated bike lanes, particularly along the Tamsui River.

8. Airport Transportation

From Taoyuan International Airport, travelers can reach Taipei via airport buses, airport MRT, or taxis. The airport MRT is the fastest option, taking passengers to Taipei Main Station in about 35 minutes.

9. EasyCard and iPass

Both EasyCard and iPass are contactless payment cards widely used in Taipei's transportation network. These cards can be used for MRT, buses, YouBike rentals, and even some convenience stores. They are convenient for frequent travelers as they offer discounted fares and save time on individual ticket purchases.

10. Traffic Tips and Considerations

Rush Hours: Taipei's rush hours typically occur on weekdays from 7:30 AM to 9:00 AM and 5:00 PM to 7:00 PM. During these times, public transportation might be crowded.

Seat-Giving Etiquette: On public transport, be mindful of priority seating designated for the elderly, disabled, and pregnant passengers.

Mobile Apps: Several mobile apps provide real-time information on public transportation schedules, routes, and traffic conditions.

CHAPTER 1

Planning Your Trip to Taipei

Visa and Entry Requirements

Visa and entry requirements for Taipei depend on the traveler's nationality and the purpose of their visit. It is essential to familiarize yourself with the necessary documentation to ensure a smooth and hassle-free entry into the city.

1. Visa-Exempt Entry

Citizens of many countries can enter Taiwan visa-free for short stays. The duration of visa-exempt stays varies by nationality but typically ranges from 30 to 90 days. Some countries under the visa-exemption program include the United States, Canada, the United Kingdom, most EU countries, Australia, New Zealand, and many others. It is crucial to check the specific visa-exempt requirements and duration for your nationality before planning your trip.

2. Visa on Arrival

For citizens of certain countries not covered by the visa-exemption program, Taiwan offers visa-on-arrival services. Travelers must meet specific criteria and provide necessary documents upon arrival at the airport or designated port of entry. Visa-on-arrival is typically granted for a shorter duration compared to visa-exempt entry.

3. Visitor Visa

If you plan to stay in Taiwan for an extended period or for purposes other than tourism, you will likely need to apply for a visitor visa before your trip. This type of visa is suitable for those visiting family or friends, pursuing business activities, attending conferences or events, or participating in academic or cultural exchange programs.

4. Application Process

Visa applications are processed through Taiwan's overseas missions, including embassies and consulates. Travelers must submit the necessary documents, which often include a passport with a minimum validity of six months, a completed visa application form, passport-sized photos, proof of sufficient funds for the duration of stay, travel itinerary, and accommodation details.

5. eVisa

Taiwan has introduced an eVisa program for travelers from certain countries. The eVisa application can be completed online, simplifying the visa application process and reducing processing time.

6. Visa Extensions

If you wish to extend your stay beyond the initially granted period, you may apply for a visa extension at the National Immigration Agency. Extensions are subject to approval and may have specific requirements depending on the purpose of the extension.

7. Work Permits and Residence Visas

For those intending to work or study in Taiwan, different visa types and work permits apply. Work permits typically require sponsorship from an employer or educational institution.

8. Important Tips

Always check the latest visa requirements and regulations from official government sources, such as the Bureau of Consular Affairs, to ensure you have the most up-to-date information.

Apply for visas well in advance of your travel dates to avoid any last-minute complications.

Keep copies of important documents, including your passport, visa, and travel itinerary, in both physical and digital formats.

Travel Budget and Currency

Understanding the travel budget and currency considerations for Taipei is essential for planning a cost-effective and enjoyable trip. Here, we'll cover various aspects related to budgeting for your Taipei travel experience.

1. Currency and Exchange Rates

The official currency of Taiwan is the New Taiwan Dollar (TWD or NT$). The currency is abbreviated as NTD when represented internationally. Banknotes and coins come in various denominations, with NT$100, NT$500, and NT$1,000 banknotes being the most commonly used. Coins are available in NT$1, NT$5, NT$10, NT$50, and NT$100 denominations.

2. Currency Exchange

Currency exchange services are readily available at international airports, major hotels, and banks throughout Taipei. Additionally, many ATMs in the city accept international debit and credit cards, providing an easy way to withdraw local currency at competitive exchange rates.

3. Credit Cards and Payment Methods

Credit cards are widely accepted in Taipei, especially in hotels, restaurants, shopping malls, and tourist attractions. Visa and Mastercard are the most commonly accepted cards, followed by JCB and American Express. However, it is advisable to carry some cash, especially for small purchases at local markets and street vendors that may not accept cards.

4. Travel Budget

Your travel budget for Taipei will depend on several factors, including accommodation preferences, dining choices, and the activities you plan to engage in. As a general guideline:

Accommodation: Taipei offers a range of accommodation options, from budget hostels to luxury hotels. Prices can vary depending on location, amenities, and the time of year. On average, budget travelers can expect to spend around NT$800 to NT$1,500 per night, while mid-range hotels may range from NT$1,800 to NT$4,000 per night.

Dining: Taipei is renowned for its diverse culinary scene, with options for all budgets. Street food and local eateries offer affordable meals, with prices ranging from NT$50 to NT$200 per meal. Dining at mid-range restaurants may cost between NT$300 to NT$800 per person, while upscale dining experiences can be more expensive.

Transportation: Taipei's efficient public transportation system is cost-effective. An MRT ride typically costs between NT$20 to NT$50, depending on the distance traveled. Buses and YouBike rentals are also budget-friendly options.

Sightseeing and Activities: Many of Taipei's attractions are either free or have affordable entrance fees. Expect to pay around NT$100 to NT$500 for admission to museums, temples, and cultural sites.

5. Saving Tips

Street Food: Taipei's night markets and street food stalls offer delicious and affordable meals, making them a budget-friendly dining option.

Free Attractions: Take advantage of Taipei's free attractions, such as exploring the city's parks, visiting temples, and attending cultural events.

Transportation Passes: Consider purchasing an EasyCard or iPass for public transportation, as they offer discounted fares and are valid on MRT, buses, and YouBike.

Shop at Local Markets: Shop for souvenirs, fresh produce, and everyday items at local markets for better prices compared to tourist-centric areas.

6. Tipping Culture

Tipping is not customary in Taipei, as service charges are often included in restaurant bills. However, it is common to round up the bill or leave small change as a gesture of appreciation for exceptional service.

Accommodation Options

Taipei offers a diverse range of accommodation options to suit every traveler's preferences and budget. From luxury hotels to budget hostels, the city caters to various needs, ensuring a comfortable stay for all visitors.

1. Luxury Hotels

For travelers seeking a touch of opulence and impeccable service, Taipei's luxury hotels are an excellent choice. Many international hotel chains have a presence in the city, offering luxurious amenities, spacious rooms, fine dining restaurants, and top-notch facilities such as spas and fitness centers. These hotels are often situated in prime locations, providing stunning city views.

2. Boutique Hotels

Boutique hotels in Taipei offer a more personalized and unique experience compared to large chain hotels. They often showcase distinctive architecture, stylish interiors, and creative design elements. These properties are typically smaller, providing an intimate and cozy ambiance. Boutique hotels are scattered throughout the city, with some located in historic neighborhoods, providing an immersive cultural experience.

3. Mid-Range Hotels

Mid-range hotels offer a balance between comfort and affordability. These hotels provide comfortable rooms and standard amenities, making them ideal for travelers seeking a comfortable stay without splurging on luxury. Mid-range hotels are widely available throughout Taipei, offering convenient access to popular attractions and public transportation.

4. Budget Accommodations

Budget travelers will find an array of affordable accommodation options in Taipei. Hostels and guesthouses are prevalent in the city, providing dormitory-style rooms or private rooms at budget-friendly prices. These accommodations are popular among backpackers and solo travelers, offering a chance to meet fellow adventurers from around the world.

5. Serviced Apartments

For extended stays or travelers seeking a home-away-from-home experience, serviced apartments in Taipei are an excellent choice.

These apartments are fully furnished with kitchen facilities, making them suitable for families or travelers who prefer self-catering options. Serviced apartments are often located in residential areas, providing a taste of local life.

6. Airbnb and Vacation Rentals

Airbnb and other vacation rental platforms offer a wide selection of private apartments and homes for short-term stays in Taipei. These rentals provide the flexibility to choose from a range of properties, allowing travelers to find accommodations that match their preferences and group size.

7. Hostels and Guesthouses

Hostels and guesthouses are prevalent in Taipei and cater to budget travelers. They offer shared dormitory-style rooms or private rooms with shared facilities, creating a social atmosphere that fosters interactions among guests. Hostels often organize social events and tours, providing opportunities to connect with other travelers.

8. Location Considerations

Xinyi District: This area is known for luxury hotels, high-end shopping, and nightlife. It is an excellent choice for those seeking a vibrant and cosmopolitan atmosphere.

Da'an District: Da'an offers a mix of upscale hotels and mid-range accommodations. It is a popular choice for its trendy cafes, boutique shops, and cultural attractions.

Zhongzheng District: This district is home to historical landmarks and government buildings, making it a convenient base for sightseeing and exploring Taipei's cultural heritage.

Wanhua District: Wanhua is famous for its historic streets and night markets. Budget travelers will find affordable accommodations in this area.

9. Booking Tips

Book in Advance: Taipei is a popular destination, so it is advisable to book accommodations in advance, especially during peak travel seasons and major events.

Read Reviews: Before booking, read reviews from previous guests to gain insights into the quality of service and facilities offered by the accommodation.

Consider Amenities: Consider the amenities and services offered by the hotel or hostel, such as breakfast, Wi-Fi, laundry facilities, and airport transfers.

10. Accommodation Safety

Taipei is considered a safe city for travelers, and its accommodations typically maintain high security standards. However, it is always wise to exercise basic precautions, such as locking valuables in the provided safe and being cautious with personal belongings.

Packing Tips and Essential Items

Packing smartly for your Taipei trip will enhance your travel experience and ensure you have everything you need for a comfortable stay. Here are some essential packing tips and items to consider for your journey.

1. Weather-Appropriate Clothing

Taipei's climate varies throughout the year, so pack clothing suitable for the season of your visit. In the summer, lightweight and breathable clothing is essential to stay comfortable in the heat and humidity. Pack shorts, T-shirts, and dresses for daytime wear. For autumn and spring, pack layers, including light jackets or cardigans, as the weather can be unpredictable. In winter, bring medium-weight clothing, sweaters, and a warm coat, as temperatures can drop.

2. Comfortable Walking Shoes

Comfortable walking shoes are a must for exploring Taipei's numerous attractions and neighborhoods. Choose footwear that provides ample support and cushioning to keep your feet comfortable during long walks and sightseeing excursions.

3. Sun Protection

Protect yourself from the strong Taiwanese sun by packing sunscreen, sunglasses, and a wide-brimmed hat. These items will help shield you from harmful UV rays, especially during outdoor activities and sightseeing tours.

4. Umbrella or Raincoat

Taipei experiences occasional rain showers, especially during the wetter months. Carry a compact travel umbrella or a lightweight raincoat to stay dry when the rain surprises you.

5. Portable Power Bank and Adapters

Ensure you have a portable power bank to keep your electronic devices charged during your adventures. Taiwan uses a Type A electrical plug with two flat parallel pins, so bring the appropriate adapter if needed.

6. Essential Documents

Remember to pack all essential travel documents, including your passport, visa, travel insurance, and any printed travel itineraries or reservations. Store copies of these documents separately from the originals for added security.

7. Medications and First Aid Kit

Pack any necessary medications and a basic first aid kit, including pain relievers, antacids, band-aids, and antiseptic ointment. Check with your doctor for any recommended vaccinations or travel health precautions before your trip.

8. Reusable Water Bottle

Stay hydrated while exploring Taipei by carrying a reusable water bottle. Taipei's tap water is safe to drink, and many public places have water dispensers where you can refill your bottle.

9. Travel Backpack or Day Bag

A travel backpack or day bag is essential for carrying your belongings during daily outings. Choose a comfortable and durable bag that can accommodate your camera, water bottle, sunscreen, and other essentials.

10. Travel Insurance

Consider purchasing comprehensive travel insurance that covers medical emergencies, trip cancellations, and lost or stolen belongings. In the event of unanticipated events, travel insurance offers comfort and financial security.

11. Language Assistance

Carry a pocket-sized English-Mandarin phrasebook or download a translation app to help bridge any language barriers during your trip. Although English is spoken in many tourist areas, knowing a few basic phrases in Mandarin can be helpful and appreciated.

12. Snacks and Refillable Containers

If you have dietary restrictions or prefer certain snacks, consider packing a few favorites for your trip. Additionally, having a reusable food container can be handy for storing leftovers or buying street food to-go.

CHAPTER 2

Top Tourist Attractions

Taipei 101

Taipei 101, formerly known as the Taipei World Financial Center, is an iconic skyscraper that dominates Taipei's skyline. Located in the Xinyi District, this architectural marvel was once the tallest building in the world and remains an emblem of Taiwan's economic prowess and modernity.

1. Architecture and Design

Designed by the renowned architect C.Y. Lee, Taipei 101 is a prime example of modern engineering and sustainable architecture. The building's design draws inspiration from traditional Asian pagodas, with its distinctive stacked tier structure symbolizing growth and prosperity. The blue-green tinted glass exterior mirrors the city's natural landscapes and the surrounding mountains.

2. Height and Observation Decks

Standing at 508 meters (1,667 feet) tall, Taipei 101 held the title of the world's tallest building from 2004 to 2010. The skyscraper consists of 101 floors above ground and five additional underground levels. Visitors can take high-speed elevators to the indoor and outdoor observation decks on the 89th and 91st floors, respectively, offering breathtaking panoramic views of Taipei and the surrounding areas.

3. Wind Damper and Engineering Marvel

To withstand typhoon winds and earthquakes common in Taiwan, Taipei 101 is equipped with a massive wind damper, known as the "Tuned Mass Damper." Suspended between the 87th and 92nd floors, this 660-ton pendulum stabilizes the building during strong winds, reducing vibrations and ensuring the safety and comfort of occupants.

4. Shopping and Dining

The lower levels of Taipei 101 house an upscale shopping mall with designer boutiques, international brands, and luxury retailers. Visitors can indulge in a shopping spree while also experiencing an array of dining options, from gourmet restaurants serving world-class cuisines to local eateries offering Taiwanese delicacies.

5. New Year's Eve Fireworks Display

Taipei 101's New Year's Eve fireworks display has become a global spectacle, attracting visitors from all over the world. The dazzling pyrotechnics illuminate the night sky, creating a breathtaking visual display that has earned Taipei international acclaim as one of the top destinations to celebrate the New Year.

6. Getting There

Taipei 101 is easily accessible via the Taipei Metro (MRT). The Xiangshan (象山) Station on the Red Line (Tamsui-Xinyi Line) is a short walk from the skyscraper. Visitors can also take advantage of various public transportation options, including buses and taxis, to reach this iconic landmark.

National Palace Museum

The National Palace Museum, located in Shilin District, is one of Taiwan's most famous cultural institutions. It houses an extensive collection of Chinese art and artifacts, making it one of the most significant museums of its kind in the world.

1. Historical Background

The National Palace Museum's roots trace back to the Forbidden City in Beijing, China, during the Ming and Qing dynasties. When the Chinese Civil War erupted, the Kuomintang (Nationalist) forces retreated to Taiwan, bringing with them a vast collection of cultural treasures to safeguard them from potential destruction. Today, these invaluable artifacts form the core of the museum's collection.

2. Artifacts and Collections

The museum's collection spans over 8,000 years of Chinese history, encompassing ceramics, calligraphy, paintings, bronzes, jades, sculptures, and rare books. Some of the most famous pieces include the Jadeite Cabbage, the Meat-shaped Stone, and the "Along the River During the Qingming Festival" painting.

3. Southern Branch

In addition to the main museum in Taipei, the National Palace Museum has a Southern Branch located in Chiayi County. The Southern Branch offers a fresh perspective on Chinese art and culture and serves as an extension of the Taipei museum.

4. Multimedia Exhibits

The museum has embraced modern technology to enhance the visitor experience. Interactive displays, multimedia presentations, and audio guides provide in-depth explanations of the artifacts and their historical significance.

5. Chang Dai-chien Gallery

The museum has a dedicated gallery for the works of Chang Dai-chien, a prominent Chinese artist known for his innovative and influential style. Visitors can appreciate his landscape paintings and artistic contributions in this specially curated space.

6. Surroundings and Gardens

The museum's surroundings are equally impressive, with serene gardens and landscapes that reflect the beauty of traditional Chinese gardens. The peaceful environment complements the cultural treasures on display, offering visitors a tranquil setting to appreciate art and history.

7. Visitor Tips

The museum is vast, so plan to spend several hours exploring the various galleries.

English audio guides are available to provide detailed explanations of the exhibits.

Check the museum's website for special exhibitions and events happening during your visit.

The museum can get crowded, especially during peak tourist seasons, so consider visiting during weekdays or early in the morning for a more relaxed experience.

Chiang Kai-shek Memorial Hall

The Chiang Kai-shek Memorial Hall, located in the heart of Taipei, is a symbolic landmark honoring the former President of the Republic of China, Chiang Kai-shek. The grandiose architecture and serene surroundings make it a significant cultural and historical site.

1. History and Significance

The memorial hall was completed in 1980, shortly after Chiang Kai-shek's death in 1975. It was built to commemorate his contributions to the development of Taiwan and to symbolize the country's transition to a democratic society.

2. Architecture and Design

The memorial hall's design is influenced by traditional Chinese architecture, featuring a white facade and a blue octagonal roof. The colors white and blue are symbolic of mourning and reflection, respectively. The structure's imposing dimensions, with its 76-meter (249-foot) tall main hall, reflect Chiang Kai-shek's significant role in Taiwan's history.

3. Main Hall and Bronze Statue

The main hall houses a bronze statue of Chiang Kai-shek seated on a throne. The statue, made of over 60 tons of bronze, measures 6 meters (20 feet) in height. It is flanked by honor guards, who perform a changing of the guard ceremony every hour, attracting numerous visitors.

4. Memorial Park and Gardens

Surrounding the memorial hall is a vast park with meticulously landscaped gardens, ponds, and cherry blossom trees. The park offers a peaceful environment for leisurely walks and quiet reflection.

5. Changing of the Guard Ceremony

The changing of the guard ceremony at the Chiang Kai-shek Memorial Hall is a solemn and impressive event. It takes place every hour from 9 a.m. to 5 p.m. The precision and formality of the ceremony attract tourists and locals alike.

6. National Concert Hall and National Theater

Adjacent to the memorial hall are the National Concert Hall and the National Theater. These venues host various cultural performances, including classical concerts, traditional Chinese music performances, and dance shows.

7. Visitor Tips

The memorial hall is open to the public, and admission is free.

Avoid visiting during extreme heat or rainy days, as the memorial hall's outdoor area is less enjoyable in unfavorable weather conditions.

The memorial hall is easily accessible by public transportation, with the Chiang Kai-shek Memorial Hall MRT station located nearby.

Longshan Temple

Longshan Temple, located in the Wanhua District, is one of the oldest and most revered temples in Taipei. This significant cultural and religious site is dedicated to various deities, making it an important spiritual center for locals and visitors alike.

1. History and Origins

Longshan Temple was originally built in 1738 by Chinese settlers from Fujian province during the Qing Dynasty. Over the years, the temple has undergone several repairs and restorations, but its historical attractiveness and spiritual value have not changed.

2. Architectural Design

The temple's architectural style showcases a blend of traditional Chinese and Taiwanese influences. It features intricately carved wooden beams, vibrant roof tiles, and ornate stone sculptures, displaying the skilled craftsmanship of its artisans.

3. Religious Significance

Longshan Temple is a multi-denominational religious site, welcoming worshippers from various religious backgrounds. Devotees come to seek blessings and guidance from a multitude of deities, including Guanyin (Goddess of Mercy), Mazu (Goddess of the Sea), and various other gods and goddesses.

4. Rituals and Activities

Visitors can observe traditional religious rituals performed by temple staff and worshippers. These rituals include lighting incense, making offerings, and praying for good fortune and protection. Fortune-telling services are also available for those seeking guidance and insights into their future.

5. Night Market Surroundings

The temple's location in the vibrant Wanhua District places it within walking distance of the historic Bopiliao Old Street and the bustling Huaxi Street Night Market. The temple's surroundings offer a glimpse of Taipei's rich history and lively street culture.

6. Festivals and Events

Longshan Temple hosts various religious festivals throughout the year, attracting large crowds and creating a lively atmosphere. The most significant celebration is the annual Longshan Temple

Festival, held on the 18th day of the first lunar month, featuring elaborate processions and cultural performances.

7. Visitor Tips

Dress modestly when visiting the temple as a sign of respect.

Be mindful of religious practices and avoid interrupting ceremonies or prayer sessions.

Photography is generally permitted, but check for any signs indicating otherwise.

The temple can get crowded, especially during festivals and weekends, so consider visiting during weekdays or early in the morning for a quieter experience.

Ximending

Ximending is a vibrant and eclectic neighborhood in the Wanhua District, renowned for its youthful energy, diverse entertainment, and lively shopping scene. Often compared to Tokyo's Harajuku and New York's Times Square, Ximending is a popular destination for locals and tourists seeking an immersive urban experience.

1. Youth Culture and Trendsetting

Ximending is at the forefront of Taiwan's youth culture and subcultures. It is a hub for creativity, fashion, and artistic expression. The area's dynamic atmosphere attracts young people and artists, making it an ideal spot to experience contemporary Taiwanese culture.

2. Shopping Paradise

Ximending is a shopaholic's paradise, offering an array of shopping options. From trendy boutiques and vintage stores to popular retail chains, visitors can find clothing, accessories, cosmetics, electronics, and much more. Ximending is especially popular among teenagers and young adults for its unique and affordable fashion offerings.

3. The Red House

The Red House, a historic octagonal building located in the heart of Ximending, is a cultural and artistic landmark. It hosts a variety of events, exhibitions, and performances, showcasing the creativity and talent of local artists.

4. Street Performances and Buskers

Ximending's streets are bustling with street performers, buskers, and live entertainment. Visitors can enjoy impromptu music performances, dance routines, magic shows, and more while exploring the area.

5. Food and Nightlife

Ximending is a gastronomic haven, offering a diverse range of dining options. From street food stalls selling traditional Taiwanese snacks to trendy cafes and international cuisine, visitors can sample a variety of delicious flavors. The area also comes alive at night, with bars, clubs, and karaoke venues providing a lively nightlife scene.

6. Cinema Street

Cinema Street is a popular spot for movie enthusiasts, with a concentration of theaters showcasing the latest blockbuster films and indie productions. It is an ideal place to catch a movie after a day of shopping and exploration.

7. The Ximen Pedestrian Area

The Ximen Pedestrian Area, the central hub of Ximending, is closed to vehicular traffic, creating a safe and vibrant pedestrian zone. The area is filled with street art, colorful decorations, and neon lights, enhancing the area's lively and youthful ambiance.

8. Getting There

Ximending is easily accessible by the Taipei Metro. The Ximen MRT Station is a major transportation hub, connecting various MRT lines and making it convenient for travelers to explore the city.

Elephant Mountain

Elephant Mountain, also known as Xiangshan, is a popular hiking destination in Taipei known for its stunning views of the city skyline and Taipei 101. It offers a rewarding outdoor experience and is a favorite spot for locals and tourists seeking a memorable sunset or night view.

1. Hiking Trail

The hiking trail to Elephant Mountain begins at the Xiangshan MRT Station and is well-marked, making it easy for visitors to find their way. The hike involves a series of stairs and steep inclines, so it is essential to wear comfortable walking shoes and bring plenty of water.

2. Scenic Views

As hikers ascend Elephant Mountain, they will be rewarded with increasingly breathtaking views of Taipei City, the Taipei Basin, and the iconic Taipei 101. The higher vantage points provide spectacular photo opportunities, especially during sunrise and sunset.

3. Sunset and Night Views

One of the best times to visit Elephant Mountain is during the late afternoon to catch the sunset. The changing colors of the sky and the sparkling city lights after dark create an enchanting scene that attracts both photographers and romantic couples.

4. Lighted Pathways

For safety and convenience, the hiking trail is equipped with well-lit pathways, allowing hikers to enjoy the nighttime views without the risk of navigating in the dark.

5. Picnic Area

At the top of Elephant Mountain, there is a designated picnic area with benches and seating, providing a perfect spot to rest and take in the scenic vistas.

6. Visitor Tips

Wear comfortable clothing suitable for hiking, and bring a light jacket in case the weather changes.

Remember to bring water and snacks to stay hydrated and energized during the hike.

During peak times, the trail can get crowded, so plan your visit accordingly.

To record the breathtaking sights, remember to bring your camera or smartphone.

Beitou Hot Springs

Beitou Hot Springs, located in the northern part of Taipei, is a natural hot spring region famous for its therapeutic and relaxing waters. The area is a serene escape from the bustling city, offering visitors a chance to unwind and rejuvenate in a tranquil natural setting.

1. Geothermal Activity

Beitou's hot springs are a result of the geothermal activity in the region, caused by the Datun Volcano Group. The mineral-rich thermal waters are believed to have healing properties and are especially beneficial for the skin and muscles.

2. Public Hot Spring Baths

Beitou is home to several public hot spring baths, including the historic Beitou Hot Spring Park, where visitors can enjoy the hot springs in an open-air setting surrounded by lush greenery. The Millennium Hot Spring and the nearby Sakuraoka Hot Spring are also popular options.

3. Private Hot Spring Hotels

For a more exclusive experience, many hotels and resorts in Beitou offer private hot spring facilities in their guest rooms. These luxurious accommodations provide an intimate and personalized hot spring experience, allowing guests to relax in privacy and comfort.

4. Beitou Library and Hot Spring Museum

Apart from the hot springs, Beitou is home to the Beitou Library, a stunning eco-friendly building with a green roof that blends harmoniously with its natural surroundings. The Beitou Hot Spring Museum is another must-visit attraction, showcasing the history and development of hot spring culture in the region.

5. Thermal Valley

The Thermal Valley, also known as Hell Valley, is a geothermal hot spring source with water temperatures reaching up to 100 degrees Celsius (212 degrees Fahrenheit). It is a striking natural wonder but is not suitable for bathing due to its extreme heat.

6. Spa and Wellness Centers

In addition to the public and private hot spring baths, Beitou offers various spa and wellness centers where visitors can indulge in therapeutic massages, aromatherapy treatments, and other spa services for a complete relaxation experience.

7. Visitor Tips

Check the operating hours and admission fees for public hot spring baths and private hot spring hotels.

Bring a bathing suit, towel, and flip-flops if visiting public hot spring baths.

Observe the hot spring etiquette, which often includes showering before entering the hot springs and refraining from using soap or shampoo while bathing.

Respect local customs and cultural norms during your visit to the hot springs.

Maokong Gondola

The Maokong Gondola is an aerial cable car system that offers a picturesque journey from the city to the tranquil mountain area of Maokong. The gondola ride provides stunning views of Taipei's landscape and is a delightful experience for nature enthusiasts and photography enthusiasts alike.

1. Scenic Route

Taipei Zoo, Taipei Zoo South, Zhinan Temple, and Maokong are the four stops on the Maokong Gondola route, which has a total length of around 4.3 kilometers (2.7 miles). Passengers may take in expansive views of the Taipei Basin, the neighboring mountains, and beautiful woods throughout the about 30-minute-long trip.

2. Taipei Zoo Station

The journey begins at the Taipei Zoo Station, where visitors can explore the Taipei Zoo before boarding the gondola. The zoo is home to a diverse collection of animals and is a family-friendly destination.

3. Zhinan Temple

The Zhinan Temple Station is a popular stop along the gondola route. The Zhinan Temple, perched on a hillside, is a significant Taoist temple with beautiful architecture and sweeping views of the city below.

4. Tea Plantations and Teahouses

Maokong is renowned for its tea plantations, producing some of Taiwan's finest oolong teas. Visitors can explore the tea fields and visit traditional teahouses to experience a traditional tea ceremony while taking in the serene mountain views.

5. Hiking Trails

Maokong offers various hiking trails for outdoor enthusiasts. The trails lead through bamboo forests, tea plantations, and scenic landscapes, providing an opportunity to connect with nature and escape the urban bustle.

6. Sunset Views

The Maokong Gondola provides an ideal vantage point to witness breathtaking sunsets over the Taipei skyline and beyond. The golden hour bathes the landscape in a warm glow, creating a memorable and romantic setting.

7. Visitor Tips

Consider purchasing a round-trip ticket for the gondola ride to enjoy the return journey with stunning views in both directions.

Check the weather forecast before planning your visit, as the gondola may be suspended in adverse weather conditions.

Wear comfortable shoes if planning to explore the hiking trails in Maokong.

Shilin Night Market

Shilin Night Market is one of Taipei's most famous and bustling night markets, drawing locals and tourists alike for its lively atmosphere, delectable street food, and diverse shopping options. It is a must-visit destination to experience Taiwan's vibrant street culture and culinary delights.

1. Food Paradise

Shilin Night Market is a paradise for foodies, offering a wide array of Taiwanese street food. From the famous stinky tofu and oyster omelet to grilled squid and bubble tea, visitors can indulge in a gastronomic feast that caters to all tastes.

2. Local Delicacies

The night market is an excellent place to sample regional specialties from all over Taiwan, making it a culinary melting pot of flavors and textures.

3. Shopping and Bargaining

Shilin Night Market offers a variety of shopping experiences, including clothing, accessories, electronics, and souvenirs. Bargaining is a common practice, so visitors can try their hand at negotiating for better prices.

4. Game Stalls and Entertainment

The market is not just about food and shopping; it also offers a range of game stalls and carnival-style attractions, providing entertainment for visitors of all ages. Test your skills and win prizes at games like shooting darts and ring tossing.

5. Live Performances

Street performances and live music add to the vibrant ambiance of Shilin Night Market. Local artists and entertainers showcase their talents, creating an enjoyable and festive atmosphere.

6. Accessories and Fashion

Shilin Night Market is a haven for fashion enthusiasts, offering trendy clothing, accessories, and stylish items at affordable prices. Fashion-forward visitors can explore the latest trends and pick up unique pieces to update their wardrobe.

7. Opening Hours

The market typically opens in the late afternoon and stays bustling until late at night, making it an ideal spot for a nighttime adventure.

8. Visitor Tips

Come hungry and ready to explore the diverse street food offerings.

Bring cash, as many stalls may not accept credit cards.

Be mindful of your belongings, as crowded night markets can be a target for pickpockets.

Wear comfortable shoes and dress casually for ease of movement.

Yangmingshan National Park

Yangmingshan National Park is a picturesque natural retreat located just outside Taipei. Known for its stunning landscapes, hot springs, and diverse flora and fauna, the park offers a refreshing escape from the urban environment.

1. Volcanic Landscapes

Yangmingshan is an active volcanic area, boasting geothermal features such as hot springs, fumaroles, and sulfur deposits. The unique volcanic landscapes make it a popular destination for nature enthusiasts and geology enthusiasts.

2. Hiking Trails

The park offers a network of well-maintained hiking trails, suitable for hikers of all levels. Popular hiking routes include the Seven Stars Peak, Xiaoyoukeng, and Qingtiangang trails, which provide breathtaking views of the surrounding mountains and Taipei City.

3. Cherry Blossom Season

During spring, usually from late February to early March, Yangmingshan is blanketed in cherry blossoms. The park becomes a floral wonderland, attracting numerous visitors who come to witness the stunning cherry blossom displays.

4. Hot Springs

Yangmingshan is home to several natural hot springs, offering visitors a chance to relax and soak in therapeutic mineral-rich waters. Hot spring facilities range from public bathhouses to private resorts.

5. Flower Clock and Flower Gardens

The Yangmingshan Flower Clock is a well-known landmark in the park, boasting colorful floral displays that change with the seasons. The Flower Gardens, such as the Zhuzihu (Bamboo Lake) and Qingtiangang, are also popular spots for flower enthusiasts.

6. Qingtiangang Grassland

Qingtiangang is a picturesque grassland area in Yangmingshan, offering a peaceful and tranquil setting for leisurely walks and picnics. The vast open space allows visitors to take in the natural beauty of the park.

7. Visitor Center and Facilities

The Yangmingshan Visitor Center provides information about the park's trails, attractions, and natural features. The park also offers various facilities, including restrooms, picnic areas, and food stalls.

8. Visitor Tips

Check weather conditions and dress accordingly, as the weather in Yangmingshan can be cooler than Taipei City.

Bring sufficient water and snacks for hiking trips, as there may not be many food options along the trails.

Respect the park's natural environment and follow guidelines to preserve the pristine landscapes.

Yangmingshan can be accessed by public transportation, making it a convenient day trip from Taipei.

CHAPTER 3

Exploring Taipei's Neighborhoods

Zhongzheng District

Zhongzheng District is a central district in Taipei, named after the former President of the Republic of China, Chiang Kai-shek, whose given name was Zhongzheng. This bustling area is known for its historical landmarks, government buildings, educational institutions, and vibrant cultural scene.

1. Historical Landmarks

Zhongzheng District is home to several significant historical landmarks that showcase Taiwan's rich heritage. Notable sites include:

National Taiwan Museum: Established in 1908, the National Taiwan Museum is the oldest museum in Taiwan and features exhibits on natural history, anthropology, and cultural artifacts.

228 Peace Memorial Park: This park commemorates the tragic 228 Incident, a violent uprising in 1947 that led to martial law and authoritarian rule. The park is a serene space for reflection and hosts events promoting peace and understanding.

Presidential Office Building: An iconic architectural symbol of Taiwan, the Presidential Office Building served as the official residence of the Governor-General of Taiwan during the Japanese colonial period and later became the Presidential Office after the end of World War II.

2. Government and Administrative Hub

Zhongzheng District houses several government buildings, including the Executive Yuan, Legislative Yuan, and Judicial Yuan, making it the administrative heart of Taiwan. Visitors can witness the functioning of Taiwan's democratic system by observing legislative sessions and exploring the government buildings' exteriors.

3. Educational Institutions

The district is also known for its prominent educational institutions, including:

National Taiwan University: Established in 1928, National Taiwan University (NTU) is the oldest and most prestigious university in Taiwan, known for its academic excellence and beautiful campus.

National Central Library: As the national library of Taiwan, the National Central Library houses a vast collection of books, documents, and multimedia resources.

4. Cultural Scene

Zhongzheng District boasts a vibrant cultural scene with numerous theaters, art galleries, and performance venues. The National Theater and Concert Hall complex hosts a wide range of cultural performances, including concerts, plays, and traditional Taiwanese opera.

5. Food and Dining

The district offers a diverse selection of dining options, from traditional Taiwanese eateries to international cuisines. Yongkang Street, known for its food stalls and restaurants, is a popular destination for food enthusiasts.

6. Transportation

Zhongzheng District is well-connected to other parts of Taipei through an extensive public transportation system. The Taipei Main Station serves as a major transportation hub, providing access to the Taipei Metro, trains, and buses.

Wanhua District

Wanhua District is one of Taipei's oldest neighborhoods, known for its rich history, vibrant night markets, and cultural attractions. Located in the western part of the city, Wanhua offers a blend of tradition and modernity, making it an intriguing destination for visitors.

1. Historic Streets and Temples

Wanhua District is home to several historic streets that offer a glimpse into Taipei's past:

Bopiliao Old Street: This well-preserved street features traditional red brick buildings from the Qing Dynasty era, providing a nostalgic ambiance and serving as a popular filming location for period dramas.

Ximending: A bustling shopping and entertainment district, Ximending is known for its youthful energy, trendy boutiques, and vibrant street culture.

Longshan Temple: As one of Taiwan's oldest and most significant temples, Longshan Temple is a major religious site attracting worshippers and visitors alike. It is dedicated to various deities, including Guanyin (Goddess of Mercy) and Mazu (Goddess of the Sea).

2. Night Markets

Wanhua District is famous for its lively night markets, where visitors can immerse themselves in the local street food culture and shopping experience:

Huaxi Street Night Market (Snake Alley): Known for its exotic offerings, this night market is famous for its snake-based dishes and traditional Chinese medicine shops.

Guangzhou Street Night Market: This bustling market offers a wide range of Taiwanese street food, local snacks, and bargain shopping.

3. Ximending Youth Culture

Ximending, a neighborhood within Wanhua District, is a hub for youth culture and fashion. It attracts young people and artists, making it an ideal spot to experience contemporary Taiwanese culture.

4. Longshan Cultural Park

Longshan Cultural Park is a renovated historic building complex that serves as a cultural and creative center. It hosts art exhibitions, performances, and workshops, showcasing the district's creative talents.

5. Transport Accessibility

Wanhua District is easily accessible by public transportation, with several MRT stations, including Ximen and Longshan Temple stations, providing convenient access to the area.

Datong District

Datong District is a charming and culturally rich area in Taipei, known for its traditional markets, historic temples, and cultural heritage. It is located near the city center and offers a glimpse into Taipei's past while embracing modern developments.

1. Dihua Street

Dihua Street is a historic street that dates back to the Qing Dynasty. It is lined with traditional shophouses selling an array of goods, including Chinese herbs, textiles, dried fruits, and traditional snacks. The street is especially vibrant during the Lunar New Year, attracting crowds looking for festive decorations and seasonal treats.

2. Cultural Attractions

Datong District is home to several significant cultural attractions:

Confucius Temple: The Taipei Confucius Temple is a serene and elegant sanctuary dedicated to Confucius, the revered Chinese philosopher. Visitors can enjoy the peaceful ambiance and admire the traditional architecture.

Baoan Temple: Baoan Temple is one of Taipei's oldest and most important temples, dedicated to Baosheng Dadi, the God of

Medicine. The temple's intricate wood carvings and ornate decorations are a testament to Taiwanese craftsmanship.

3. Traditional Markets

Datong District is known for its traditional markets, where visitors can experience authentic local life:

Ningxia Night Market: Ningxia Night Market is a must-visit destination for food enthusiasts. It offers a variety of Taiwanese snacks, seafood, and regional delicacies.

Dalongdong Bao'an Temple Market: This day market, located near the Baoan Temple, features stalls selling fresh produce, local products, and snacks.

4. Modern Developments

Despite its historical charm, Datong District has undergone modern developments, including the construction of new residential and commercial buildings, providing a mix of old and new architecture.

5. Transport Accessibility

Datong District is well-connected to other parts of Taipei through the Taipei Metro, with several MRT stations, such as Daqiaotou and Shuanglian, offering easy access to the area.

Xinyi District

Xinyi District is Taipei's modern and upscale district, known for its towering skyscrapers, luxury shopping malls, and vibrant nightlife. It is a bustling area that caters to both business travelers and tourists seeking an upscale experience.

1. Taipei 101

Xinyi District is home to Taipei 101, an iconic skyscraper and a symbol of Taiwan's economic prowess.From 2004 until 2010, Taipei 101 held the record for being the highest skyscraper in the world. Still an artistic creation.

2. Luxury Shopping

The district is a paradise for luxury shopping, with upscale malls like Taipei 101 Mall and Breeze Xinyi offering international designer brands, high-end boutiques, and exclusive products.

3. Nightlife and Entertainment

Xinyi District comes alive at night with its lively nightlife scene. The area offers trendy bars, nightclubs, and entertainment venues, making it a popular spot for locals and tourists looking for a fun night out.

4. Xinyi Financial Center

Apart from Taipei 101, the Xinyi Financial Center includes other modern skyscrapers housing offices, hotels, and corporate headquarters, making it Taipei's commercial hub.

5. Elephant Mountain

Xinyi District is the gateway to Elephant Mountain (Xiangshan), a popular hiking destination that offers stunning views of Taipei City and Taipei 101. The trek is particularly well-liked during dawn and dusk.

6. Eslite Bookstore - Xinyi Store

Eslite Bookstore is a renowned Taiwanese bookstore chain, and its Xinyi flagship store is a cultural and literary landmark. The store is open 24/7 and offers a vast collection of books, magazines, and cultural products.

7. World-class Dining

Xinyi District boasts a diverse selection of dining options, from high-end restaurants serving international cuisines to local eateries offering Taiwanese delicacies.

8. Transport Accessibility

Xinyi District is easily accessible by public transportation, with several MRT stations, including Taipei 101/World Trade Center and City Hall, providing convenient access to the area.

Da'an District

Da'an District is a dynamic and diverse neighborhood in Taipei, known for its leafy streets, fashionable boutiques, and artistic vibe. It is a popular destination for locals and expats seeking a vibrant and cosmopolitan atmosphere.

1. Yongkang Street

Yongkang Street is a trendy and bustling street in Da'an District, lined with a variety of cafes, restaurants, and specialty shops. It is a popular spot for foodies looking to savor international cuisines and artisanal delights.

2. Da'an Forest Park

Da'an Forest Park is a sprawling urban park that offers a tranquil retreat from the city's hustle and bustle. The park features jogging paths, picnic areas, and a large pond, providing a peaceful environment for relaxation and recreation.

3. Creative and Artistic Scene

Da'an District is known for its creative and artistic scene, with many independent art galleries, design studios, and creative spaces. The area fosters a lively cultural community and hosts various art exhibitions and cultural events.

4. Technology and Innovation

Da'an District is home to numerous tech startups and innovation hubs, contributing to Taipei's reputation as a center of technological advancement in Asia.

5. National Taiwan University (NTU)

Da'an District is also home to National Taiwan University (NTU), Taiwan's most prestigious university. The campus's vibrant atmosphere and cultural events add to the district's dynamic energy.

6. Dongmen Market

Dongmen Market is a traditional market in Da'an District, offering fresh produce, local snacks, and traditional Taiwanese products. It is a great place to experience the local culture and sample authentic Taiwanese cuisine.

7. Fashion Boutiques and Vintage Stores

Da'an District is a haven for fashion enthusiasts, with a wide range of fashion boutiques and vintage stores selling unique and stylish clothing and accessories.

8. Transport Accessibility

Da'an District is well-connected to other parts of Taipei through public transportation, with several MRT stations, such as Da'an Park and Technology Building, providing easy access to the area.

Beitou District

Beitou District is a charming and picturesque district in northern Taipei, known for its natural hot springs, lush greenery, and serene landscapes. It offers a relaxing escape from the bustling city, making it a popular destination for those seeking a tranquil retreat.

1. Hot Springs

Beitou is famous for its natural hot springs, which have been enjoyed for centuries for their healing properties. The district offers a variety of hot spring facilities, ranging from public bathhouses to private resorts and hotels.

2. Beitou Hot Spring Museum

The Beitou Hot Spring Museum is a historic building that was once a public bathhouse during the Japanese colonial period.

Today, it serves as a museum, providing visitors with insights into the history and culture of hot springs in Beitou.

3. Thermal Valley

Thermal Valley, also known as Hell Valley, is a geothermal hot spring source with water temperatures reaching up to 100 degrees Celsius (212 degrees Fahrenheit). It is an impressive natural wonder, but not suitable for bathing due to its extreme heat.

4. Yangmingshan National Park

Beitou District is adjacent to Yangmingshan National Park, offering visitors the opportunity to explore the park's lush landscapes, hiking trails, and beautiful flower fields.

5. Plum Garden

Plum Garden is a historic residence that once belonged to Lin Hsien-tang, a renowned calligrapher and artist. The garden features traditional Japanese-style architecture and a beautiful garden, providing a peaceful environment for visitors.

6. Xinbeitou and Qingnian Road

Xinbeitou is a lively area in Beitou known for its hot spring hotels, restaurants, and shops. Qingnian Road, adjacent to Xinbeitou, is a popular spot for food enthusiasts, with numerous eateries offering a variety of Taiwanese and international cuisines.

7. Transport Accessibility

Beitou District is easily accessible by public transportation, with the Xinbeitou MRT station providing convenient access to the area.

Songshan District

Songshan District is a dynamic and diverse neighborhood in Taipei, known for its mix of modern developments, cultural attractions, and local charm. It offers a range of experiences for both locals and tourists.

1. Raohe Street Night Market

Raohe Street Night Market is one of Taipei's most famous night markets, offering a wide array of Taiwanese street food, local snacks, and unique souvenirs. For those who like eating, it is a must-visit location.

2. Ciyou Temple

Ciyou Temple is a striking Taoist temple known for its colorful architecture and intricate carvings. It is dedicated to Mazu, the

Goddess of the Sea, and serves as a significant religious and cultural landmark.

3. Rainbow Bridge

Rainbow Bridge is an iconic pedestrian bridge that spans across the Keelung River, connecting Songshan District to the Xinyi District. It is beautifully illuminated at night, providing a picturesque backdrop for nighttime strolls.

4. Wufenpu Garment Wholesale Area

Wufenpu is a bustling garment wholesale area, offering a wide selection of trendy and affordable clothing. It is a favorite shopping spot for locals and tourists seeking fashionable clothing at bargain prices.

5. Songshan Cultural and Creative Park

Songshan Cultural and Creative Park is a vibrant hub for arts, design, and creativity. It hosts various exhibitions, events, and markets, showcasing the works of local artists and designers.

6. Eslite Spectrum Songyan Store

Eslite Spectrum Songyan Store is a multi-level lifestyle complex that houses a bookstore, boutique shops, a performance space, and various dining options. It offers a unique and sophisticated shopping and cultural experience.

7. Taipei City Hall

Songshan District is home to Taipei City Hall, a prominent government building and a symbol of the district's administrative significance.

8. Transport Accessibility

Songshan District is well-connected to other parts of Taipei through public transportation, with several MRT stations, such as Songshan and Houshanpi, providing convenient access to the area.

CHAPTER 4

Cultural and Historical Sites

Taiwanese Temples and Religious Sites

Taiwanese temples and religious sites are an integral part of the island's cultural heritage and spiritual life. Rooted in a mix of traditional Chinese folk religion, Buddhism, and Taoism, these places of worship are not only important for religious practices but also serve as cultural and historical landmarks.

1. Longshan Temple

Located in Wanhua District, Longshan Temple is one of the most renowned and oldest temples in Taipei. Built-in 1738, the temple is dedicated to various deities, including Guanyin (Goddess of Mercy) and Mazu (Goddess of the Sea). Its intricate wood carvings, stone sculptures, and vibrant roof decorations showcase traditional Taiwanese temple architecture. Visitors can witness devotees burning incense, making offerings, and praying, immersing themselves in the local religious customs.

2. Xingtian Temple

Xingtian Temple, situated in Zhongshan District, is dedicated to Guangong (Lord Guan), a famous general and deity revered for loyalty, righteousness, and protection. The temple's distinctive red facade and traditional architecture make it an eye-catching religious site. The temple attracts many worshippers seeking blessings, especially for success and prosperity in business and personal endeavors.

3. Confucius Temple

The Taipei Confucius Temple, located in Datong District, pays tribute to Confucius, the esteemed Chinese philosopher and educator. The temple's serene environment and classical Chinese architecture make it a tranquil oasis in the city. It serves as a place for cultural education and conducts ceremonies honoring Confucius, especially during Confucius's birthday on September 28.

4. Baoan Temple

Baoan Temple, situated in Datong District, venerates Baosheng Dadi, the God of Medicine. The temple's stunning craftsmanship, elaborate carvings, and delicate roof ornaments highlight the beauty of traditional Taiwanese temple art. Baoan Temple is also known for its annual pilgrimage, attracting thousands of devotees to celebrate the deity's birthday.

5. Dajia Jenn Lann Temple

Located in Dajia District, this temple is renowned for its grand annual religious procession during the Dajia Mazu Pilgrimage. It is one of Taiwan's largest religious events, attracting millions of participants and spectators. The procession involves carrying the statue of Mazu, the sea goddess, on a palanquin, with participants chanting and offering blessings along the way.

6. Zushi Temple

Zushi Temple, situated in Sanxia District, is dedicated to Xuantian Shangdi, a deity associated with protection and martial arts. The temple's intricate carvings and unique dragon-shaped columns exemplify the exquisite craftsmanship of Taiwanese temple art. The annual Sanxia Zushi Temple Pilgrimage attracts both locals and tourists to witness this religious and cultural spectacle.

7. Temples in Jiufen and Jinguashi

The historic towns of Jiufen and Jinguashi in New Taipei City are dotted with several charming temples. Jiufen's Chaotian Temple and Jinguashi's Shinto Shrine are popular religious sites worth exploring while delving into the region's fascinating history and heritage.

8. Religious Festivals

Taiwan's religious festivals are vibrant and colorful celebrations that reflect the island's cultural diversity and spiritual beliefs. Major festivals include Lunar New Year, Ghost Month, Mazu's Birthday, and the Mid-Autumn Festival. During these occasions, temples come alive with elaborate decorations, processions, and traditional performances, offering visitors an opportunity to experience Taiwan's rich religious and cultural traditions.

9. Temple Etiquette

When visiting Taiwanese temples and religious sites, it is essential to observe proper etiquette and respect local customs:

Cover your shoulders and knees when you dress modestly.

Before going inside the main prayer room, take off your shoes.

Refrain from taking photos during ceremonies or while people are praying.

Participate in rituals only if invited, and avoid touching religious objects.

When offering incense, use both hands to hold the incense sticks and bow as a gesture of respect.

Be mindful of noise and maintain a quiet demeanor to not disturb worshippers.

Historical Landmarks and Museums

Taipei's rich history and cultural heritage are well-preserved in its historical landmarks and museums. These sites offer visitors an insightful journey through Taiwan's past, from its indigenous roots to colonial rule and modern developments.

1. National Palace Museum

The National Palace Museum, located in Shilin District, is Taiwan's most iconic museum, housing one of the world's most extensive collections of Chinese art and artifacts. The museum boasts over 700,000 pieces, including ancient ceramics, paintings, calligraphy, bronzes, and jade carvings. Many of these treasures were brought to Taiwan during the Chinese Civil War to protect them from destruction.

2. Chiang Kai-shek Memorial Hall

The Chiang Kai-shek Memorial Hall, located in Zhongzheng District, is a prominent historical landmark and a symbol of Taiwan's political history. The grand white building houses a bronze statue of Chiang Kai-shek, the former President of the Republic of China. The hall's surrounding gardens and large square are popular spots for locals and tourists to relax and enjoy cultural events and performances.

3. 228 Peace Memorial Park and Museum

The 228 Peace Memorial Park, situated in Zhongzheng District, commemorates the tragic 228 Incident in 1947, a pivotal event in Taiwan's history. The park features sculptures, memorials, and a peaceful pond, offering visitors a space for reflection and remembrance. The 228 Peace Memorial Museum provides an in-depth historical account of the incident, fostering understanding and reconciliation.

4. Taipei City Walls and Bopiliao Old Street

The remnants of Taipei's historical city walls and the Bopiliao Old Street in Wanhua District offer a glimpse into the city's Qing Dynasty past. Bopiliao Old Street's well-preserved architecture and red-brick buildings create a nostalgic atmosphere, attracting both history enthusiasts and filmmakers seeking period drama settings.

5. Taiwan 101 Historical Monument

Located in Dadaocheng, the Taiwan 101 Historical Monument is a beautiful red-brick building that was originally a tea-processing plant during the Japanese colonial period. Today, it houses a tea museum and cultural center, showcasing Taiwan's tea industry and traditions.

6. Beitou Hot Spring Museum

The Beitou Hot Spring Museum, situated in Beitou District, was once a public bathhouse during the Japanese colonial era. Now a museum, it provides insights into the history and culture of hot springs in Taiwan. The building's architecture combines Japanese and Western elements, adding to its historical significance.

7. Taipei Story House

Taipei Story House, located in Zhongshan District, is a historic European-style mansion built during the Japanese colonial period. The museum exhibits artifacts from the early 20th century, offering visitors a glimpse into Taipei's past as an emerging modern city.

8. Lin An Tai Historical House and Museum

Lin An Tai Historical House, situated in Zhongshan District, is a traditional Chinese courtyard house that showcases traditional architecture and landscaping. The museum exhibits various cultural relics, making it an educational stop for those interested in traditional Taiwanese lifestyle and design.

9. Historical Themed Villages

Taipei's surrounding areas feature several historical themed villages, such as Sanxia Old Street and Jiufen, which offer visitors the opportunity to experience well-preserved old streets, unique architecture, and traditional crafts.

Traditional Taiwanese Arts and Crafts

Taiwan's artistic heritage and traditional craftsmanship are celebrated through various arts and crafts that have been passed down through generations. Exploring these art forms provides insight into the island's cultural richness and creative spirit.

1. Taiwanese Pottery and Ceramics

Taiwanese pottery and ceramics have a long history, dating back thousands of years. Areas like Yingge in New Taipei City are famous for their pottery culture. Visitors can watch skilled artisans creating pottery and purchase intricately designed teapots, bowls, vases, and other ceramic products as souvenirs.

2. Taiwanese Calligraphy and Painting

Calligraphy and painting hold a significant place in Taiwanese culture. Locals often practice calligraphy as a form of meditation and self-expression. Traditional ink paintings depict natural scenes, landscapes, flowers, and birds, often reflecting the beauty of Taiwan's natural environment.

3. Taiwanese Tea Culture

Taiwanese tea culture is deeply rooted in the island's history and lifestyle. Taiwan produces some of the finest teas globally, including oolong tea, black tea, and green tea. Visitors can participate in tea ceremonies, learn about tea processing, and taste various teas in tea houses and plantations across the island.

4. Taiwanese Handicrafts

Taiwanese handicrafts encompass a wide range of traditional art forms, such as weaving, embroidery, bamboo crafts, and wood carving. Indigenous tribes, especially, have a rich tradition of crafting exquisite textiles, baskets, and wooden sculptures.

5. Taiwanese Puppetry

Taiwanese puppetry, known as budaixi, is a traditional art form that involves puppet shows accompanied by music and storytelling. Puppet theaters in Taiwan offer performances featuring historical legends, mythological stories, and humorous skits.

6. Taiwanese Festivals and Performing Arts

Taiwanese festivals and performing arts play a crucial role in preserving the island's cultural heritage. From lion and dragon dances during Lunar New Year to traditional Taiwanese opera performances and folk dances, these art forms reflect the vibrant spirit of Taiwanese culture.

7. Traditional Music and Instruments

Taiwanese traditional music includes a variety of regional styles and instruments. The erhu (a two-stringed bowed instrument), the guzheng (a plucked zither), and the pipa (a four-stringed lute) are some of the instruments commonly associated with Taiwanese folk music.

8. Aboriginal Arts and Crafts

Taiwan's indigenous tribes maintain their unique cultural heritage through their arts and crafts. Intricate beadwork, weaving, and wooden carvings are just a few examples of the traditional crafts that showcase the tribes' creativity and craftsmanship.

Preservation and Promotion of Taiwanese Arts and Crafts

The Taiwanese government and various organizations actively promote and preserve traditional arts and crafts through workshops, exhibitions, and cultural events. These initiatives aim to pass down traditional knowledge to future generations and foster a greater appreciation for Taiwan's cultural heritage.

CHAPTER 5

Outdoor Activities in Taipei

Hiking and Nature Trails

Taipei, surrounded by lush mountains and abundant natural beauty, offers numerous hiking and nature trails for outdoor enthusiasts to explore. Whether you're a seasoned hiker or a casual nature lover, these trails cater to various skill levels and provide an opportunity to immerse yourself in Taiwan's stunning landscapes.

1. Yangmingshan National Park

Yangmingshan National Park, located just north of Taipei, is a hiker's paradise. The park offers a wide range of trails, from easy walks to more challenging hikes. One of the most popular routes is the Seven Star Mountain (Qixing Mountain) trail, which rewards hikers with breathtaking views of the surrounding mountains and Taipei City. Other notable trails in Yangmingshan include Xiaoyoukeng, where you can witness fumaroles and hot springs, and Datun Mountain, known for its diverse flora and fauna.

2. Elephant Mountain (Xiangshan)

Located near Taipei 101, Elephant Mountain is a favorite among both locals and tourists for its relatively short but rewarding hike. The trail takes about 20-30 minutes to climb, and at the summit, you're treated to panoramic views of Taipei City, Taipei 101, and the surrounding mountains. The best time to hike Elephant Mountain is during late afternoon or sunset when you can capture stunning cityscape photos.

3. Four Beasts Mountains (Sìshòu Shān)

The Four Beasts Mountains, also known as the Four Beasts Scenic Area, is a network of trails located in the southeastern part of Taipei. The four peaks—Elephant Mountain, Tiger Mountain, Leopard Mountain, and Lion Mountain—resemble their respective animal shapes when viewed from certain angles. The hike offers beautiful views of Taipei City and the Keelung River.

4. Maokong Trails

The Maokong area, famous for its tea plantations and tea houses, also offers delightful hiking trails. The trails wind through the lush greenery and provide peaceful retreats from the bustling city. You can combine a visit to Maokong Gondola with a hike, making it a memorable day trip.

5. Pingxi District Trails

The Pingxi District, known for its sky lantern festivals, also offers scenic hiking trails. The Shifen Waterfall Trail leads to a stunning waterfall surrounded by picturesque landscapes. Other trails in the area include the Sandiaoling Waterfall Trail and the Wanggu Waterfall Trail, which offer opportunities to explore more of Taiwan's natural beauty.

6. Wulai Trails

Wulai, a popular mountainous area not far from Taipei, boasts beautiful hiking trails. The Wulai Waterfall Trail leads to a majestic waterfall, and the Yunxian Waterfall Trail takes you through scenic forests and streams. Wulai's trails offer a chance to experience the indigenous culture and connect with nature.

7. Visitor Tips

Before embarking on any hike, check the weather conditions and prepare accordingly. Wear appropriate footwear, clothing, and bring sufficient water and snacks.

Some trails may require permits or have restricted access during certain seasons, so be sure to check with local authorities or visitor centers.

Respect the natural environment and follow the principles of "Leave No Trace" to help preserve Taiwan's beautiful landscapes for future generations.

Consider joining guided hiking tours or hiring a local guide for a more enriching experience and to ensure your safety.

Cycling and Biking Routes

Cycling and biking have become increasingly popular in Taipei, thanks to the city's efforts to promote eco-friendly transportation and recreational activities. With designated bike lanes and scenic routes, cyclists can explore Taipei's urban and natural wonders on two wheels.

1. Riverside Bike Paths

One of the best ways to enjoy cycling in Taipei is along the city's extensive riverside bike paths. The Keelung River, Tamsui River, and Danshui River offer dedicated bike lanes that span for kilometers, providing a smooth and safe cycling experience. Along these paths, you can enjoy views of the river, bridges, and surrounding landscapes.

2. Tamsui Bike Path

The Tamsui Bike Path is a popular route that stretches from Tamsui Fisherman's Wharf to Bali, passing through scenic spots like Lover's Bridge and Fort San Domingo. The path offers a mix of riverside views, coastal scenery, and historical sites.

3. Dadaocheng Wharf Bike Path

This bike path runs along the Dadaocheng Wharf and offers views of the Tamsui River and the Guandu Bridge. The area is known for its historical buildings and cultural heritage, making it a delightful route for history enthusiasts.

4. Taipei Riverside Park Bike Paths

The Taipei Riverside Park, located along the Keelung River, provides a series of interconnected bike paths. It's a perfect spot for leisurely biking, jogging, or having a riverside picnic. The park is particularly beautiful during cherry blossom season and in the evening when the city lights reflect on the water.

5. Yangmingshan Bike Trails

For more adventurous cyclists, Yangmingshan National Park offers challenging bike trails with beautiful views. The Qixing Mountain Trail is a popular choice, providing an exhilarating ride up the mountain and a rewarding sense of accomplishment at the summit.

6. Taipei City Biking Tour

The Taipei City Government has introduced the "YouBike" rental system, which allows visitors to easily rent bikes from various locations throughout the city. This initiative has made biking a convenient and eco-friendly way to explore Taipei's streets and neighborhoods.

7. Visitor Tips

Check the weather and air quality before embarking on a biking adventure, as Taiwan's weather can be unpredictable.

Wear appropriate safety gear, such as helmets and reflective clothing, especially if cycling during the evening.

Be cautious of traffic, especially when sharing roads with vehicles. Always follow traffic rules and signals.

Don't forget to take breaks and stay hydrated during your cycling journey.

River Cruises and Boat Tours

Taipei's waterways offer an alternative perspective to the city's urban landscape. River cruises and boat tours provide a relaxing and scenic experience, allowing you to enjoy the city's skyline and surrounding nature from a different angle.

1. Tamsui River Cruise

A Tamsui River Cruise is a popular choice for visitors seeking a leisurely boat ride along the river, providing views of the Tamsui River's picturesque shores. The cruise takes you from Tamsui Fisherman's Wharf to the Taipei Fish Market, with opportunities to see popular attractions like the Tamsui Lover's Bridge and Fort San Domingo.

2. Keelung River Sightseeing Cruise

The Keelung River Sightseeing Cruise offers a tranquil journey through the heart of Taipei. The cruise departs from Dajia Riverside Park and travels along the Keelung River, passing by iconic landmarks like Taipei Bridge and the Miramar Ferris Wheel.

3. Sunset Cruises

Several operators offer sunset cruises on the Tamsui River, providing a romantic and enchanting experience. The serene atmosphere, accompanied by the beautiful colors of the setting sun, creates an unforgettable moment for couples and photographers.

4. Bitan Boat Tour

Bitan, also known as Xindian, is a charming riverside area with a large lake. A boat tour on Bitan Lake allows you to enjoy the peaceful surroundings, paddle past picturesque bridges and pavilions, and appreciate the lush greenery of the area.

5. Baishawan Beach Boat Tour

For those looking to escape the city's hustle and bustle, Baishawan Beach, located in New Taipei City, offers boat tours to explore the rugged coastline, sandy beaches, and crystal-clear waters. The boat tour provides an opportunity to spot local wildlife and appreciate Taiwan's natural beauty.

6. Yehliu Geopark Boat Tour

While not in Taipei City itself, Yehliu Geopark, located along Taiwan's northern coast, is easily accessible for a day trip. The geopark boat tour takes visitors along the coast, showcasing unique rock formations, including the famous "Queen's Head" rock.

7. Private Boat Rentals

For a more intimate experience, consider renting a private boat or joining a small group tour for a customized river cruise experience. These tours offer flexibility in terms of route and timing, allowing you to tailor the experience to your preferences.

Picnic Spots and Parks

Taipei boasts an abundance of parks and green spaces where visitors and locals alike can enjoy picnics, outdoor activities, and relaxation amid nature.

1. Da'an Forest Park

Da'an Forest Park is a vast urban park in Da'an District, offering a peaceful retreat from the bustling city. The park features lush greenery, picturesque ponds, and walking paths, providing the perfect setting for picnics and leisurely strolls. There are also areas for exercising, playing sports, and even a large children's playground.

2. Dajia Riverside Park

Dajia Riverside Park, located along the Keelung River, is a popular spot for picnicking and outdoor recreation. The park's large open spaces, bike paths, and riverside views make it a favorite among locals for family gatherings and relaxing afternoons.

3. Xinsheng Park

Xinsheng Park is a charming park in Zhongshan District, featuring beautiful cherry blossom trees during the blooming season. It's a great spot for a springtime picnic surrounded by the pink petals of cherry blossoms.

4. Taipei Expo Park

The Taipei Expo Park, situated in Yuanshan District, is a spacious park that hosted the Taipei International Flora Expo in 2010. The park offers various themed gardens, including the beautiful

Yuanming Yuan Garden, providing an ideal setting for picnics amid vibrant floral displays.

5. Taipei Botanical Garden

The Taipei Botanical Garden, adjacent to the Presidential Office Building, is a delightful escape with diverse plant species, walking trails, and historical buildings. Visitors can find a quiet spot for a picnic amid the lush greenery and charming ponds.

6. Huashan 1914 Creative Park

Huashan 1914 Creative Park, formerly a winery during the Japanese colonial period, has been transformed into an artistic and cultural hub. The park features charming red-brick buildings, art exhibitions, and creative workshops, providing a unique picnic spot for those looking to combine art and leisure.

7. Beitou Park

Located in Beitou District, Beitou Park is famous for its hot springs and offers a serene environment for a relaxing picnic. The park's verdant landscape and shaded paths provide a soothing escape from city life.

8. Bitan (Xindian) Riverside Park

Bitan Riverside Park, situated near Xindian District, is a popular spot for picnics and outdoor activities. The park's riverside setting, with its beautiful views of Bitan Lake and the surrounding mountains, makes it a favorite location for locals and visitors to unwind and enjoy a leisurely meal.

9. Visitor Tips

Be sure to pick up any litter and dispose of it responsibly to help maintain the cleanliness of the parks and picnic spots.

Consider bringing reusable containers and utensils to minimize waste during your picnic.

Check for any park regulations or guidelines regarding picnicking and activities to ensure you are following local rules.

Some parks may have barbecue areas or designated picnic spots, so be mindful of where you choose to set up your picnic.

Don't forget to pack sunscreen, insect repellent, and plenty of water to stay hydrated during your outdoor adventure.

CHAPTER 6

Culinary Delights in Taipei

Iconic Taiwanese Dishes

Taiwanese cuisine is a delightful fusion of flavors influenced by the island's indigenous roots, Chinese traditions, and Japanese and Southeast Asian culinary influences. From mouthwatering street food to sumptuous meals in restaurants, Taipei offers a plethora of iconic Taiwanese dishes that are sure to tantalize your taste buds.

1. Beef Noodle Soup

Considered Taiwan's national dish, Beef Noodle Soup is a must-try delicacy in Taipei. The dish features tender beef, stewed in a rich and savory broth with aromatic spices, and served with chewy wheat noodles. The broth's depth of flavor and the tenderness of the beef make it a comfort food cherished by locals and visitors alike.

2. Xiao Long Bao

Xiao Long Bao, or soup dumplings, are a favorite among food enthusiasts. These delicate steamed dumplings are filled with flavorful pork or other meat, and a savory soup broth. When biting into the dumpling, be sure to savor the burst of rich broth and succulent meat.

3. Oyster Omelet

A beloved Taiwanese street food, Oyster Omelet is a delicious combination of eggs, small oysters, and tapioca starch, fried to a crispy perfection. The dish is topped with a savory sauce and garnished with fresh cilantro. The contrasting textures of the crispy omelet and tender oysters create a delightful culinary experience.

4. Gua Bao

Also known as Taiwanese hamburgers, Gua Bao consists of fluffy steamed buns filled with tender braised pork belly, pickled mustard greens, cilantro, and ground peanuts. The sweet and savory flavors meld together to create a mouthwatering treat that packs a punch of taste in each bite.

5. Scallion Pancake

Scallion Pancake is a popular Taiwanese street snack loved by locals and tourists alike. These flaky and savory pancakes are made with dough, layered with scallions and oil, and pan-fried to perfection. It's a simple yet flavorful treat that's often enjoyed as a quick breakfast or snack.

6. Bubble Tea

Bubble Tea, or Boba Tea, is a globally popular Taiwanese drink that originated in Taipei. It's a sweet and creamy milk tea beverage with chewy tapioca pearls (boba) at the bottom. You can find an extensive variety of flavors and toppings to customize your bubble tea experience.

7. Stinky Tofu

Stinky Tofu is a polarizing yet iconic Taiwanese street food known for its strong aroma. The fermented tofu is deep-fried to create a crispy exterior while retaining a soft and flavorful interior. Locals often enjoy it with a side of pickled vegetables and a dash of chili sauce.

8. Iron Eggs

A popular snack in Taiwan, Iron Eggs are quail eggs stewed in a mixture of soy sauce, spices, and tea leaves. The slow cooking process gives them a chewy texture and a savory flavor, making them a tasty and convenient snack.

9. Taiwanese Hot Pot

Taiwanese Hot Pot is a communal dining experience that involves cooking various ingredients in a simmering broth at the table. The wide selection of fresh meats, vegetables, seafood, and noodles allows diners to customize their hot pot experience. It's a social and delicious meal shared with family and friends.

10. Pineapple Cake

Pineapple Cake is a beloved Taiwanese pastry often served as a souvenir to visitors. The buttery and crumbly pastry is filled with sweet pineapple jam, creating a delightful balance of flavors.

Must-Try Street Food

Taipei's vibrant street food scene is a feast for the senses, with bustling night markets and food stalls offering an array of delectable treats. Sampling these mouthwatering street foods is a quintessential part of the Taipei experience.

1. Shilin Night Market

Shilin Night Market is Taipei's largest and most famous night market, drawing locals and tourists alike. It's a paradise for foodies, offering an abundance of street food stalls with everything from grilled squid and oyster vermicelli to stinky tofu and mango shaved ice.

2. Raohe Street Night Market

Raohe Street Night Market is another popular night market that boasts a fantastic selection of street food. Don't miss out on the famous black pepper buns (hu jiao bing), filled with juicy minced pork and seasoned with aromatic spices.

3. Ningxia Night Market

Ningxia Night Market is a hidden gem for food enthusiasts. The market is known for its wide variety of traditional Taiwanese snacks and delicacies, including Taiwanese oyster vermicelli, coffin bread, and oyster omelet.

4. Shida Night Market

Located near National Taiwan Normal University, Shida Night Market offers a vibrant food scene catering to the student population. You can find a mix of local and international flavors, including Korean barbecue, Thai street food, and Taiwanese desserts.

5. Tonghua Night Market

Tonghua Night Market is a favorite among locals, offering a more relaxed atmosphere compared to the bustling crowds of larger night markets. Here, you can savor grilled seafood, tempura, and braised pork rice.

6. Jinzhou Street

Jinzhou Street is a popular destination for Taiwanese breakfast dishes. Start your day with savory soy milk, youtiao (Chinese crullers), and dan bing (egg pancake).

7. Huaxi Street Tourist Night Market

Also known as Snake Alley, Huaxi Street Night Market is known for its exotic offerings, including snake soup and snake blood alcohol, believed to have medicinal properties.

8. Ningxia Road

Ningxia Road is another hotspot for delectable street food. Try the pepper meat buns, oyster omelet, and Taiwanese sausages, which are grilled to perfection.

9. Guangzhou Street

Guangzhou Street Night Market is a lively spot for trying various Taiwanese snacks, including fresh seafood, tempura, and mochi.

10. Ximending

Although not a traditional night market, Ximending is a bustling shopping district with numerous street food vendors. Explore its vibrant streets and try local favorites like stinky tofu and bubble tea.

Night Markets and Food Stalls

Night markets are an integral part of Taiwanese culture, offering a treasure trove of delicious street food, affordable shopping, and lively entertainment. These vibrant markets are a feast for the senses and a must-visit for any Taipei traveler.

1. Shilin Night Market

Arguably the most famous night market in Taipei, Shilin Night Market is a paradise for foodies and shoppers alike. Its bustling alleys are lined with food stalls selling a wide variety of Taiwanese snacks and delicacies. From oyster omelets and grilled squid to fried chicken and bubble tea, the choices are endless. Apart from food, Shilin Night Market also offers clothing, accessories, and various trinkets at bargain prices.

2. Raohe Street Night Market

Raohe Street Night Market is one of the oldest night markets in Taipei and is known for its lively atmosphere. The iconic Rainbow Bridge at the entrance sets the tone for a colorful and exciting experience. As you stroll along the market, you'll encounter tempting food stalls serving delicacies such as pepper buns, stinky tofu, and sesame oil chicken. Don't miss the chance to try the famous "black pepper bun," which is filled with succulent minced pork and seasoned with fragrant spices.

3. Ningxia Night Market

Ningxia Night Market is a favorite among locals for its authentic Taiwanese snacks and traditional dishes. The market is relatively compact, making it easy to navigate. Here, you'll find popular dishes like oyster omelet, oyster vermicelli, and braised pork rice. It's a great place to indulge in some genuine Taiwanese flavors.

4. Tonghua Night Market

Tonghua Night Market is a hidden gem located near Linjiang Street. This market offers a more laid-back atmosphere compared to some of the larger and busier night markets. As you explore the market, be sure to try the savory grilled seafood, tempura, and mouthwatering braised pork rice.

5. Huaxi Street Tourist Night Market

Huaxi Street Night Market, often referred to as "Snake Alley," is one of Taipei's most unique night markets. While it offers a variety of Taiwanese street food, it's also known for its exotic offerings, including snake soup and snake blood alcohol, believed to have medicinal properties.

6. Liaoning Night Market

Located near Zhongshan Junior High School MRT Station, Liaoning Night Market is a smaller market but packs a punch in terms of flavors. The market is particularly famous for its deep-fried delights, such as crispy chicken and tempura. You'll also find plenty of fruit stands offering refreshing and juicy treats.

7. Guangzhou Street Night Market

Guangzhou Street Night Market offers a diverse array of snacks and treats to delight your taste buds. Be sure to try the pepper meat buns, oyster omelet, and Taiwanese sausages, which are grilled to perfection and bursting with flavor.

8. Ningxia Road Night Market

Ningxia Road Night Market is a small and cozy market known for its delicious Taiwanese street food. Here, you can savor various local snacks, including fresh seafood, tempura, and mouthwatering mochi.

9. Ximending

Ximending is a bustling shopping district that offers a wide range of entertainment and dining options. While it's not a traditional night market, the streets are filled with street food vendors offering local favorites like stinky tofu, bubble tea, and fried chicken. It's a great place to explore the vibrant atmosphere of Taipei's youth culture.

10. Shida Night Market

Located near National Taiwan Normal University, Shida Night Market caters to the student population and offers a mix of local and international flavors. The market is a great place to try Korean barbecue, Thai street food, and Taiwanese desserts.

Themed Restaurants and Cafes

In addition to its diverse culinary scene, Taipei is also home to an array of themed restaurants and cafes that cater to various interests and preferences. These unique dining establishments offer not only delicious food but also immersive experiences that make your meal even more memorable.

1. Modern Toilet Restaurant

One of Taipei's most famous themed restaurants, the Modern Toilet Restaurant is a quirky and fun dining experience. The restaurant's interior is designed to resemble a bathroom, with toilet-shaped seats and sinks as tables. Diners are served food in dishes that resemble toilet bowls and drink from urinal-shaped glasses. Despite the unusual theme, the restaurant serves a variety of delicious hot pot and Taiwanese dishes.

2. Hello Kitty Kitchen and Dining

For fans of Hello Kitty, this restaurant is a dream come true. The Hello Kitty Kitchen and Dining restaurant features everything

Hello Kitty, from the decor to the food presentation. Diners can enjoy a menu of adorable Hello Kitty-themed dishes, including desserts shaped like the iconic character's face.

3. Barbie Café

Located in the Zhongxiao Fuxing shopping district, the Barbie Café is a pink paradise inspired by the iconic doll. The cafe's interior is adorned with Barbie dolls and memorabilia, creating a whimsical and nostalgic atmosphere. The menu offers a range of stylish and colorful dishes that pay tribute to Barbie's glamorous lifestyle.

4. Alice is Coming

Alice in Wonderland fans will delight in the whimsical ambiance of Alice is Coming. The restaurant features decor inspired by Lewis Carroll's classic tale, with elements like oversized teacups and playing cards. The menu includes creative dishes with names and presentations that reflect the enchanting world of Wonderland.

5. Ninja New York

Ninja New York brings the mystique and allure of ancient Japanese ninjas to Taipei. The restaurant offers a theatrical dining experience, where servers dressed as ninjas perform acrobatic tricks and deliver meals with flair. The menu features a fusion of

Japanese and Western dishes, making for a unique and entertaining culinary adventure.

6. Jay Chou's Mr. J Restaurant

Owned by Taiwanese pop icon Jay Chou, Mr. J Restaurant reflects the singer's artistic flair and love for music. The restaurant features chic and stylish decor, and the menu offers a fusion of Western and Asian cuisines. The ambiance and menu reflect Jay Chou's personal tastes and creative vision.

7. Café Hoho

Café Hoho is a whimsical café that caters to animal lovers, especially those who adore hedgehogs. The café allows visitors to interact with adorable hedgehogs while enjoying a cup of coffee. The hedgehogs are kept in a comfortable and safe environment, and customers can feed, pet, and take photos with them.

8. Themed Cafés in Ximending

Ximending is a hub for themed cafes, and visitors can find a range of unique concepts. These themed cafes cater to various interests, including anime, manga, gaming, and movies. Whether you're a fan of a particular anime series or simply love the idea of a themed dining experience, Ximending has something to offer.

9. Cat Cafés

Cat cafés have become a global trend, and Taipei boasts several charming cat cafés where visitors can relax and enjoy a cup of coffee or tea while interacting with friendly feline companions. These cafés provide a calm and cozy atmosphere, making them a popular spot for cat lovers and those seeking a moment of tranquility.

10. VR Cafés

As technology enthusiasts continue to explore the world of virtual reality, Taipei has embraced the trend with VR cafés. These cafes offer VR gaming experiences and simulations, allowing visitors to immerse themselves in exciting virtual worlds while enjoying drinks and snacks.

CHAPTER 7

Shopping in Taipei

Popular Shopping Districts

Taipei is a shopaholic's paradise, offering an impressive array of shopping districts catering to diverse tastes and budgets. From bustling night markets to upscale malls, each shopping area in Taipei has its unique charm and specialty.

1. Ximending

Ximending is Taipei's most famous shopping district, known for its vibrant atmosphere and youthful energy. This pedestrian-friendly area is a haven for fashion lovers, with numerous boutiques, streetwear shops, and trendy fashion outlets. You'll also find an abundance of entertainment options, including theaters, street performances, and themed cafes. Ximending is a hub for pop culture, making it a favorite spot for both locals and tourists.

2. Zhongxiao Dunhua

Zhongxiao Dunhua is a chic and trendy shopping district with a mix of international brands and local boutiques. The area is renowned for its upscale fashion stores, stylish cafes, and unique concept shops. Fashionistas and design enthusiasts will appreciate the diverse selection of clothing, accessories, and lifestyle products available here.

3. Zhongshan Metro Mall

Located underground and connected to the Zhongshan Metro Station, the Zhongshan Metro Mall is a shopping haven for budget-conscious shoppers. The mall features a wide variety of stores selling affordable clothing, accessories, electronics, and more. It's an excellent place to shop for stylish yet reasonably priced items.

4. Shida Road

Near National Taiwan Normal University, Shida Road is a popular shopping area among the younger crowd. The road is lined with boutiques, thrift stores, and indie fashion shops, offering a unique selection of clothing and accessories. Shida Road is a great place to find one-of-a-kind pieces that reflect Taipei's hip and creative culture.

5. Breeze Center

Breeze Center is an upscale shopping complex in Taipei, featuring a curated selection of international luxury brands and designer stores. The mall also houses department stores, a gourmet food market, and a wide range of restaurants and cafes. Breeze Center is the perfect destination for a luxury shopping experience.

6. Taipei 101 Mall

Located within the iconic Taipei 101 skyscraper, the Taipei 101 Mall is a high-end shopping destination. It boasts an impressive collection of luxury brands, designer boutiques, and fine dining options. The mall's luxurious interior and sophisticated ambiance make it a favorite among luxury shoppers.

7. Nanmen Market

Nanmen Market, located in Wanhua District, is a bustling market known for its budget-friendly clothing and accessories. The market offers a wide range of affordable clothing, shoes, bags, and fashion accessories, making it a popular destination for bargain hunters.

8. East Metro Mall

Connected to the Zhongxiao Fuxing Metro Station, East Metro Mall is another underground shopping area with a variety of stores selling fashion, accessories, and cosmetics. It's a convenient spot for shopping, especially during inclement weather.

9. Shilin Night Market

While primarily known for its delicious street food, Shilin Night Market also offers a vibrant shopping experience. The market features a range of stalls selling clothing, accessories, shoes, and trinkets at bargain prices. It's a great place to find trendy and affordable fashion items.

10. Dihua Street

Dihua Street is a historic market area with a rich heritage. It's famous for its traditional Chinese medicine shops, herbal remedies, and a variety of dried goods and spices. The street also houses stores selling fabrics, textiles, and traditional Taiwanese snacks, making it an interesting and culturally significant shopping destination.

Traditional Markets and Bazaars

Embracing Taiwan's cultural heritage, Taipei's traditional markets and bazaars offer an authentic and vibrant shopping experience. These markets are deeply rooted in Taiwanese culture and are essential places to explore local customs and flavors.

1. Shilin Night Market

Shilin Night Market is Taipei's largest and most famous night market, attracting locals and tourists alike. The market is renowned for its delicious street food, ranging from the iconic stinky tofu and oyster omelet to scallion pancakes and bubble tea. Besides the culinary delights, Shilin Night Market also offers a variety of stalls selling clothing, accessories, and novelty items.

2. Raohe Street Night Market

Raohe Street Night Market is another popular night market in Taipei, offering a delightful mix of local delicacies and traditional Taiwanese snacks. As you stroll along the market, you'll find vendors selling mouthwatering dishes such as pepper buns, braised pork rice, and sesame oil chicken.

3. Ningxia Night Market

Ningxia Night Market is a gem hidden in the bustling city. This compact night market is beloved by locals for its authentic Taiwanese street food and local specialties. Some must-try items include oyster omelet, Taiwanese sausage, and oyster vermicelli.

4. Tonghua Night Market

Tonghua Night Market is a local favorite that offers a relaxed and laid-back shopping experience. The market is known for its diverse food selection, including tempura, squid soup, and delicious grilled seafood. Tonghua Night Market is a great place to mingle with locals and savor authentic Taiwanese flavors.

5. Linjiang Night Market

Linjiang Night Market, also known as Tonghua Night Market, is a smaller market with a cozy and welcoming atmosphere. The market offers a variety of local snacks and dishes, such as oyster omelets, Taiwanese fried chicken, and shaved ice desserts.

6. Huaxi Street Night Market

Huaxi Street Night Market, famously known as "Snake Alley," is one of Taipei's oldest night markets. While it offers a range of traditional Taiwanese street food, the market is also known for its exotic offerings, such as snake soup and snake blood alcohol.

7. Jianguo Holiday Flower Market

The Jianguo Holiday Flower Market is a charming market specializing in fresh flowers, plants, and gardening supplies. It's a great place to pick up vibrant blooms and unique plants to brighten up your space. The market's cheerful atmosphere and colorful displays are a treat for the senses.

8. Liaoning Night Market

Liaoning Night Market is a hidden gem located near the Zhongshan Junior High School MRT Station. The market offers a range of affordable clothing, accessories, and souvenirs, making it a favorite shopping spot for budget-conscious travelers.

9. Dihua Street

Dihua Street, steeped in history, is a traditional market that dates back to the Qing Dynasty. It's a fascinating place to explore the city's cultural heritage and purchase traditional Chinese herbs, dried goods, and snacks. Dihua Street is especially vibrant during festivals like the Lunar New Year, where locals flock to buy festive decorations and traditional treats.

10. Nanmen Market

Nanmen Market is a bustling market located in Wanhua District, offering an authentic local shopping experience. The market is known for its budget-friendly clothing, shoes, bags, and fashion accessories. It's a great place to shop for stylish items at affordable prices.

Trendy Boutiques and Designer Stores

For those seeking cutting-edge fashion and high-quality design, Taipei's trendy boutiques and designer stores are a treasure trove of contemporary styles and exquisite craftsmanship.

1. Zhongxiao Dunhua

Zhongxiao Dunhua is an upscale shopping district known for its chic boutiques and designer stores. It's a favorite among fashion-forward locals and trendsetters. Here, you'll find a mix of international luxury brands, local designers, and stylish concept stores.

2. Da'an District

Da'an District is home to a myriad of boutique stores, ranging from high-end luxury brands to independent fashion labels. The district's wide streets and tree-lined boulevards make it a pleasant area for leisurely shopping and exploring unique boutiques.

3. Breeze Center

Breeze Center is an elegant shopping complex that houses a curated selection of international luxury brands and high-end designer stores. The mall's sophisticated ambiance and well-appointed displays cater to discerning shoppers looking for exclusive fashion pieces.

4. Dongmen

Dongmen is a vibrant neighborhood with an artistic and bohemian vibe. The area is a treasure trove of indie boutiques, vintage shops, and local designers. Dongmen is perfect for those seeking one-of-a-kind fashion pieces and unique accessories.

5. Xinyi District

Xinyi District is Taipei's central business and commercial hub, hosting upscale malls and luxury boutiques. The area surrounding Taipei 101, in particular, features designer stores from renowned fashion houses and high-end international brands.

6. Songshan Cultural and Creative Park

The Songshan Cultural and Creative Park is a hub for artistic and innovative designs. Housed in a converted tobacco factory, the park showcases a range of trendy boutiques and design shops. It's a great place to discover cutting-edge fashion, unique accessories, and creative lifestyle products.

7. Dunhua South Road

Dunhua South Road is known for its fashionable shops and boutiques offering a mix of modern and classic styles. You'll find a range of contemporary fashion brands, accessory stores, and trendy shoe shops along this stylish boulevard.

8. Yongkang Street

Yongkang Street is famous for its hip and trendy vibe, with an abundance of boutique stores, stylish cafes, and chic eateries. The area is known for its modern fashion boutiques, offering cutting-edge designs and up-and-coming fashion labels.

9. Neihu District

Neihu District is emerging as a new fashion hub in Taipei, featuring a range of trendy boutiques and concept stores. The area caters to young and fashion-conscious locals, offering a mix of contemporary fashion, accessories, and lifestyle products.

10. Ximen

Ximen is a bustling shopping district with a youthful and energetic vibe. The area features an eclectic mix of boutique stores, vintage shops, and indie labels. Ximen is popular among young shoppers looking for unique and trendy fashion pieces.

Souvenirs and Local Crafts

Taking home souvenirs and local crafts is a wonderful way to commemorate your trip to Taipei and support local artisans. Whether it's traditional Taiwanese handicrafts or modern design pieces, Taipei has a diverse range of unique gifts to offer.

1. Jianguo Holiday Flower Market

Apart from fresh flowers and plants, Jianguo Holiday Flower Market also offers a selection of arts and crafts, including handmade accessories, pottery, and small trinkets. These items make for thoughtful and nature-inspired gifts to take back home.

2. Dihua Street

Dihua Street is a treasure trove for those seeking traditional Taiwanese crafts and souvenirs. Here, you'll find a variety of items, including Chinese tea sets, traditional fabrics, calligraphy brushes, and festive decorations. Dihua Street is especially vibrant during festivals like the Lunar New Year, making it a great place to buy traditional holiday souvenirs.

3. Chiang Kai-shek Memorial Hall Gift Shop

The Chiang Kai-shek Memorial Hall's gift shop offers a selection of unique souvenirs and crafts inspired by Taiwanese culture and history. Visitors can find beautiful tea sets, delicate ceramics, and traditional handicrafts, making it a perfect place to pick up meaningful gifts.

4. Taipei Expo Park Gift Shops

The Taipei Expo Park hosts various themed gardens and exhibitions, each offering unique souvenirs related to the flora and cultural themes. From potted plants and gardening tools to artistic home decor, the gift shops at the Taipei Expo Park provide a wide range of green and creative gifts.

5. Sun Yat-sen Memorial Hall Gift Shop

The Sun Yat-sen Memorial Hall's gift shop offers a selection of traditional Taiwanese souvenirs, including calligraphy brushes, lanterns, and handcrafted jewelry. The items reflect Taiwan's cultural heritage and make for meaningful and artistic gifts.

6. Handmade Markets and Art Fairs

Taipei hosts various handmade markets and art fairs throughout the year, featuring the works of local artisans and designers. These events offer a unique shopping experience and the chance to discover one-of-a-kind crafts, fashion pieces, and artistic creations.

7. Shilin Night Market

In addition to its delicious street food, Shilin Night Market also offers stalls selling unique souvenirs and local crafts. Visitors can find everything from trendy fashion accessories to cute stationery and traditional Taiwanese snacks to take back home.

8. Yongkang Street

Yongkang Street, known for its trendy boutiques, also houses shops selling artisanal products and locally made crafts. Visitors can find unique fashion accessories, handmade leather goods, and creative lifestyle items that make for distinctive souvenirs.

9. Taipei Fine Arts Museum Gift Shop

The Taipei Fine Arts Museum's gift shop offers a selection of art-related souvenirs, including prints, postcards, and art books. The shop also sells creative design products inspired by the museum's exhibitions, providing a unique opportunity to take home a piece of Taiwan's contemporary art scene.

10. Themed Souvenir Shops

Various tourist attractions in Taipei have their own themed souvenir shops, offering a range of unique gifts related to the site's history or cultural significance. These shops are great places to find exclusive souvenirs that can't be found elsewhere.

CHAPTER 8

Nightlife and Entertainment

Bars and Pubs

Taipei's nightlife is vibrant and diverse, and the city boasts a wide selection of bars and pubs where locals and tourists alike can unwind and socialize. Whether you're looking for a laid-back atmosphere to enjoy a craft beer or a stylish rooftop bar with stunning city views, Taipei has something to suit every taste.

1. Attic

Located in Da'an District, Attic is a popular speakeasy-style bar known for its craft cocktails and cozy ambiance. The bar's skilled mixologists concoct creative and innovative drinks, making it a favorite spot for cocktail enthusiasts. Attic's dimly lit interior and vintage decor create an intimate setting for a relaxed evening.

2. Revolver

Revolver is an iconic bar in Taipei, known for its live music, friendly staff, and extensive selection of beers and spirits. The bar's interior is adorned with quirky decorations, including vintage memorabilia and album covers. With a regular lineup of local and international bands, Revolver is a go-to spot for music lovers.

3. Ounce

Ounce is a hidden gem in Taipei, a cozy cocktail bar specializing in whiskey-based drinks. The bar's knowledgeable bartenders are passionate about whiskey and can guide you through their impressive selection of rare and unique bottles. Ounce is an ideal destination for connoisseurs seeking a sophisticated and refined drinking experience.

4. Barcode

Barcode is a modern and trendy bar located in Xinyi District, known for its stylish decor and chic ambiance. The bar offers a wide variety of cocktails, wines, and spirits. With its DJ spinning tunes, Barcode is a favorite among young professionals and party-goers looking for a fun night out.

5. BeerGeek Taipei

BeerGeek Taipei is a haven for craft beer enthusiasts, offering an extensive selection of local and international craft beers on tap. The bar's rotating taps feature a diverse range of beer styles, from IPAs and stouts to sours and barrel-aged brews. It's a great place to discover Taiwan's burgeoning craft beer scene.

6. The Pawnshop

The Pawnshop is a unique and quirky bar in the heart of Taipei. Hidden behind a nondescript storefront, this speakeasy-style bar features an old-world charm with vintage decorations and furniture. The Pawnshop's skilled bartenders serve up creative cocktails, making each visit a delightful surprise.

7. On Tap

On Tap is a lively sports bar that attracts a mix of locals and expats. The bar boasts an impressive selection of beers on tap and screens live sports events from around the world. With its casual and friendly atmosphere, On Tap is an excellent place to catch up on sports and enjoy a relaxed night out with friends.

8. The Drunken Master Whisky Bar

Located in the Zhongshan District, The Drunken Master Whisky Bar is a paradise for whiskey aficionados. The bar offers a vast array of whiskey from various regions and countries, allowing guests to savor rare and hard-to-find bottles. The knowledgeable staff can help you explore different flavors and find your perfect dram.

9. Beer & Cheese Social House

Beer & Cheese Social House is a cozy and laid-back bar that combines the pleasures of craft beer with gourmet cheese offerings. The bar's curated beer selection pairs perfectly with their cheese platters, providing a unique and enjoyable experience for beer and cheese enthusiasts.

10. Fourplay Cuisine & Bar

Fourplay Cuisine & Bar is a trendy spot in the Da'an District, offering creative cocktails and delicious fusion dishes. The bar's stylish interior and rooftop terrace create a chic and contemporary setting for a night of socializing and indulgence.

Nightclubs and Dancing Venues

For those who enjoy dancing and a vibrant nightlife scene, Taipei offers an array of nightclubs and dancing venues where you can dance the night away to the latest beats and tunes.

1. OMNI

OMNI is one of Taipei's most popular nightclubs, located in the bustling Xinyi District. The club's state-of-the-art sound system and impressive visual effects create an immersive and electrifying atmosphere. OMNI hosts top local and international DJs, drawing in crowds of party-goers looking for an unforgettable night of dancing and entertainment.

2. Myst

Myst is a sprawling nightclub complex with multiple rooms and dance floors, each offering different music genres and atmospheres. Located in Xinyi District, Myst is a magnet for dance enthusiasts, offering a wide range of music styles, including electronic dance music (EDM), hip-hop, and pop.

3. Elektro

Elektro is a vibrant and energetic nightclub that caters to EDM and electronic music lovers. The club's dynamic lighting and energetic vibes make it a popular destination for young locals and tourists seeking a high-energy dance experience.

4. Luxy

Luxy is an iconic nightclub in Taipei, known for its upscale and exclusive ambiance. The club attracts a glamorous crowd, with a strict dress code and door policy. Inside, you'll find multiple levels and rooms, each offering a different style of music and setting.

5. Triangle

Triangle is a popular nightclub and live music venue located in the bustling Ximending area. The club features a diverse lineup of live performances, DJs, and themed parties, making it a favorite among locals and international visitors.

6. AI

AI is a trendy nightclub located in the heart of Taipei. With its stylish decor, cutting-edge lighting, and sound system, AI provides an immersive clubbing experience. The club hosts popular local and international DJs, ensuring an energetic and lively atmosphere.

7. Funky Club

As the name suggests, Funky Club is a vibrant venue that celebrates funky and groovy beats. The club hosts themed parties and events, with a focus on soul, funk, and disco music. It's a great place to dance to classic tunes and enjoy a retro-inspired night out.

8. Lava

Lava is a lively nightclub in Taipei that caters to a diverse audience. The club's various rooms offer different music genres, from hip-hop and R&B to electronic dance music. Lava is known for its energetic dance floors and dynamic performances.

9. APA Mini

APA Mini is a popular nightclub in Taipei, attracting a young and energetic crowd. The club features a mix of live performances and DJ sets, providing an eclectic and exciting nightlife experience.

10. Barcode

Barcode, mentioned earlier as a bar, transforms into a bustling nightclub in the later hours. With its stylish decor, resident DJs, and dance floor, Barcode offers a seamless transition from a relaxing bar atmosphere to a lively nightclub setting.

Live Music and Concerts

Taipei's live music scene is thriving, with a plethora of venues showcasing diverse musical genres and performances. From intimate jazz clubs to large concert halls, Taipei offers an eclectic selection of live music experiences.

1. Legacy Taipei

Legacy Taipei is a popular live music venue that hosts a wide range of performances, including concerts by local bands, international acts, and themed music events. The venue's intimate setting and excellent acoustics make it a favorite among music enthusiasts.

2. The Wall

The Wall is an iconic live music venue in Taipei, known for its support of the local indie music scene. The venue hosts concerts and performances by both established and up-and-coming bands and artists. The Wall is a platform for music discovery and a place to experience the creativity and diversity of Taiwan's music culture.

3. Riverside Live House

Riverside Live House is located by the Tamsui River and is a hub for live music performances. The venue showcases a mix of genres, including rock, indie, folk, and alternative music. Riverside Live House's relaxed atmosphere and riverside views create a unique and memorable setting for live music experiences.

4. Blue Note Taipei

Blue Note Taipei is a branch of the renowned jazz club franchise, offering world-class jazz performances in a sophisticated setting. The club hosts jazz musicians from Taiwan and around the world, providing an exceptional jazz experience for music connoisseurs.

5. Underworld

Underworld is a well-known venue in Taipei's music scene, focusing on rock, metal, and alternative music genres. The club hosts concerts and gigs by local and international bands, making it a go-to spot for fans of heavy and alternative music.

6. Riverside Café

Riverside Café is a laid-back venue with a riverside location, featuring live performances and open mic nights. The cafe offers a mix of music styles, including acoustic, indie, and folk, making it a great place to relax and enjoy live music in a casual environment.

7. Legacy Mini

As an extension of Legacy Taipei, Legacy Mini is a smaller venue that provides a more intimate space for music performances. The venue showcases emerging artists and bands, offering a cozy and up-close experience for concert-goers.

8. A House

A House is a unique live music venue that combines music with a cozy and homey atmosphere. The venue is housed in a converted residential building, creating an intimate and warm setting for live music performances.

9. APA House

APA House is a live music venue known for its diverse music lineup, including rock, jazz, blues, and folk. The venue often hosts themed music nights and special events, attracting music lovers with different tastes.

10. PIPE Live Music

PIPE Live Music is a multifunctional live music venue that hosts concerts, parties, and events. The venue features a spacious stage and a large standing area, providing a lively and energetic atmosphere for music performances.

Theater and Performances

In addition to its vibrant music scene, Taipei offers an array of theatrical performances and cultural shows that showcase the richness of Taiwanese arts and performing arts.

1. National Theater and Concert Hall

The National Theater and Concert Hall are two iconic venues in Taipei, located next to each other in Liberty Square. The National Theater hosts various traditional performing arts, such as Peking opera and Taiwanese opera. The Concert Hall, on the other hand, is a renowned venue for classical music performances and orchestral concerts.

2. TaipeiEYE

TaipeiEYE is a cultural performance center that offers traditional Taiwanese arts and theatrical shows. The performances feature elements of Peking opera, Taiwanese opera, martial arts, acrobatics, and puppetry. TaipeiEYE provides an immersive and educational experience for visitors interested in Taiwanese culture and performing arts.

3. U-Theatre

U-Theatre is a Taiwanese performance group that combines traditional art forms with contemporary aesthetics. The group specializes in Zen drumming performances, blending percussion with dance and visual elements to create a mesmerizing and spiritual experience.

4. Experimental Theater

Located within the National Theater and Concert Hall complex, the Experimental Theater hosts innovative and experimental performances, including contemporary dance, theater, and multimedia shows. The theater is a platform for emerging artists and avant-garde productions.

5. Cloud Gate Theater

Cloud Gate Theater is a world-renowned contemporary dance company based in Taipei. Known for its breathtaking performances and artistic choreography, Cloud Gate Theater showcases the beauty and grace of Taiwanese contemporary dance.

6. Red Theater

Red Theater is a unique venue that specializes in traditional Taiwanese puppetry. The theater's performances feature elaborate puppetry techniques and storytelling, providing a captivating glimpse into Taiwan's puppetry heritage.

7. National Taichung Theater

Although located in Taichung City, the National Taichung Theater is worth mentioning as it hosts various high-quality performances and international productions. The avant-garde architecture and modern facilities of the theater provide a stunning backdrop for diverse artistic performances.

8. The Red House

The Red House is a historic building in Ximending that hosts various cultural and artistic events. The venue features a mix of theatrical performances, art exhibitions, and cultural festivals, making it a lively hub for the arts in Taipei.

9. Novel Hall for Performing Arts

Novel Hall for Performing Arts is a modern theater located in Xinyi District, featuring a mix of performances, including musicals, plays, dance shows, and concerts. The theater's diverse lineup attracts a wide range of audiences, from theater enthusiasts to music lovers.

10. TaipeiEYE Storyteller's Party

TaipeiEYE Storyteller's Party is a unique theatrical experience that combines traditional Taiwanese storytelling with modern performance elements. The show presents classic stories and legends from Taiwanese culture, bringing them to life with music, dance, and colorful visuals.

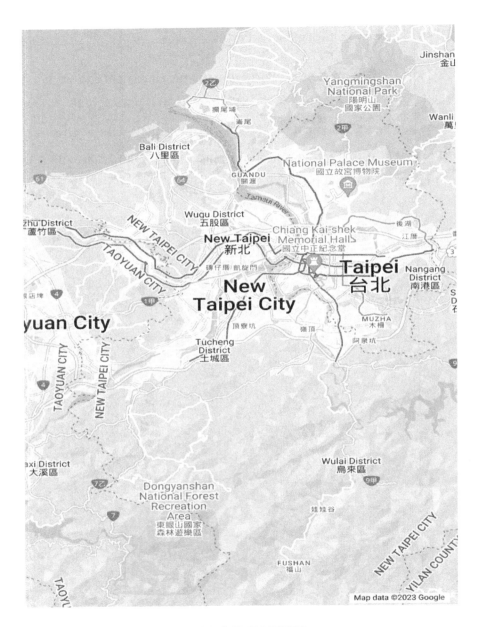

MAP OF TAIPEI

CHAPTER 9

Practical Information and Safety Tips

Emergency Numbers and Healthcare

Emergency Numbers

When traveling to Taipei, it's essential to be aware of the emergency contact numbers in case of any unforeseen circumstances. The emergency services in Taipei are efficient and reliable, providing assistance in various situations.

1. Ambulance and Medical Emergencies: If you require urgent medical assistance or ambulance service, dial 119. The operators are trained to handle medical emergencies and will dispatch the appropriate medical assistance to your location promptly.

2. Fire Emergency: In the event of a fire or any fire-related emergency, dial 119. The fire department will respond swiftly to address the situation and provide assistance.

3. Police: If you encounter a crime or need to report an emergency that requires police intervention, dial 110. The police in Taipei are well-trained and responsive to public safety matters.

Healthcare

Taipei boasts excellent healthcare facilities and medical services. The city's hospitals are equipped with modern technologies and staffed by highly trained medical professionals. However, as a foreign traveler, it's essential to be aware of the following healthcare aspects:

1. Travel Insurance: Before traveling to Taipei, ensure that you have comprehensive travel insurance that covers medical emergencies, hospitalization, and medical evacuation if needed. Most international insurance policies are accepted in Taipei, but it's best to confirm with your insurance provider beforehand.

2. Medical Facilities: Taipei has several reputable hospitals and medical centers that cater to both locals and tourists. Some well-known hospitals include Taipei Veterans General Hospital, National Taiwan University Hospital, and Mackay Memorial Hospital.

3. Language Barrier: While many medical professionals in Taipei speak English, it's still beneficial to have essential medical information translated into Mandarin or have a translation app handy. It's also helpful to carry a copy of your medical history and any existing medical conditions in case of an emergency.

4. Pharmacies: Pharmacies are abundant in Taipei, and you can find both Western and traditional Chinese medicine options. Many common over-the-counter medications are readily available, but if you require specific prescription medication, ensure you have enough supply for your trip.

5. COVID-19 Precautions: In light of the COVID-19 pandemic, it's crucial to stay informed about the latest travel advisories and regulations related to the virus. Adhere to local health guidelines, wear masks in public areas if required, and maintain social distancing to protect yourself and others.

Language and Communication

1. Mandarin Chinese: The official language of Taiwan is Mandarin Chinese. While most locals in Taipei speak Mandarin fluently, there are also speakers of other languages, including Taiwanese Hokkien and indigenous languages.

2. English: English is widely taught in schools, and many people in Taipei, especially in tourist areas and businesses, have a basic understanding of English. You can communicate with hotel staff, restaurant servers, and tour operators in English with relative ease.

3. Language Barrier: Despite the prevalence of English speakers, there may still be instances of communication challenges, especially in more rural areas or when dealing with older

individuals. Learning a few basic phrases in Mandarin, such as greetings and common expressions, can be helpful and appreciated by locals.

4. Translation Apps: If you find it challenging to communicate in Mandarin, consider using translation apps on your smartphone. There are various apps available that can help you translate written text or facilitate conversations with locals.

Cultural Etiquette and Customs

1. Respect for Elders: In Taiwanese culture, showing respect for elders is highly valued. When interacting with older individuals, address them with appropriate honorifics and gestures of respect.

2. Bowing: While handshakes are becoming more common, especially in business settings, the traditional greeting is a slight bow. A nod of the head is also considered a polite gesture.

3. Shoes Off Indoors: It's customary to remove your shoes before entering someone's home, certain restaurants, and temples. Look for a row of shoes outside the entrance as an indication that you should do the same.

4. Chopstick Etiquette: When dining in Taipei, be mindful of chopstick etiquette. Don't stick chopsticks vertically into a bowl of

rice, as it resembles a funeral ritual. Additionally, avoid pointing chopsticks at others while speaking.

5. Gift-Giving: If invited to someone's home, it's customary to bring a small gift as a token of appreciation. Gifts should be modest, and it's polite to present them with both hands.

6. Tipping: Tipping is not a common practice in Taipei, as it is already included in the bill or service charge. However, if you receive exceptional service, leaving a small tip as a token of gratitude is appreciated.

7. Public Behavior: Public displays of affection are generally not common in Taiwanese culture. It's also considered impolite to raise your voice or show anger in public.

8. Queuing: Taiwanese people are known for their orderly behavior, and queuing is taken seriously. Always queue up in an organized manner and wait for your turn patiently.

9. Photography: When taking photos of people, especially at religious or cultural sites, always ask for permission first. Some places may have restrictions on photography, so be mindful of any signage or guidelines.

10. Bargaining: Bargaining is not commonly practiced in Taipei, except in certain situations like flea markets or street vendors. In most stores and restaurants, the prices are fixed.

Safety Precautions and Travel Warnings

1. Street Safety: Taipei is generally a safe city, but like any urban area, it's essential to stay vigilant, especially in crowded areas. Keep an eye on your things and avoid bringing large amounts of cash or expensive items.

2. Traffic Safety: When crossing the street, always use designated pedestrian crossings and obey traffic signals. Taiwanese drivers can be aggressive, so exercise caution when walking or cycling near roads.

3. Earthquakes: Taiwan is located in a seismic region, and earthquakes can occur. Familiarize yourself with earthquake safety measures, such as finding sturdy shelter and staying away from glass windows during a quake.

4. Typhoons: Typhoon season in Taiwan is from June to November. Pay attention to weather forecasts and advisories, and follow instructions from local authorities in case of a typhoon warning.

5. Drinking Water: Tap water in Taipei is generally safe to drink, but some people prefer to drink bottled or filtered water. If unsure, stick to bottled water to avoid any potential gastrointestinal issues.

6. Scams and Pickpocketing: While Taipei is relatively safe, be cautious of scams targeting tourists, such as overpriced tours or counterfeit goods. Keep an eye on your belongings in crowded places to prevent pickpocketing.

7. Political Demonstrations: Taiwan has a vibrant democracy, and political demonstrations can occur. If you encounter a protest, stay away from the area and follow local news for updates on the situation.

8. Travel Warnings: Before traveling to Taipei, check the latest travel advisories and warnings issued by your government. These advisories provide information on safety and security concerns for specific regions.

9. Sun Protection: Taipei can get hot and sunny, so remember to wear sunscreen, a hat, and sunglasses to protect yourself from the sun's rays, especially during outdoor activities.

10. Emergency Contact Information: Always carry essential contact information, such as the address and phone number of your hotel, the nearest embassy or consulate, and your travel insurance provider.

CONCLUSION

In conclusion, Taipei is a dynamic and captivating city that offers an enriching travel experience for visitors. From its iconic landmarks and vibrant neighborhoods to its rich cultural heritage and delectable cuisine, Taipei has something to offer every traveler. Whether you're exploring the bustling night markets, immersing yourself in traditional Taiwanese arts, or savoring the city's iconic dishes, Taipei promises unforgettable moments at every turn. With its modern infrastructure, friendly locals, and a wealth of attractions, Taipei stands as a remarkable destination that seamlessly blends tradition and innovation. So, pack your bags, embark on a journey of discovery, and let Taipei's charm and allure captivate your heart and soul.

Printed in Great Britain
by Amazon

28564738R00086